Studies on Contemporary Europe

Edited by
PROFESSOR ALAN S. MILWARD
University of Manchester Institute of Science and Technology

4

The Integration of the
European Economy since 1815

Studies on Contemporary Europe

The Integration of the European Economy since 1815

SIDNEY POLLARD

Professor of Economic and Social History, University of Sheffield

University Association for Contemporary European Studies

George Allen & Unwin

GEORGE ALLEN & UNWIN LTD
40 Museum Street, London WC1A 1LU

© University Association for Contemporary European Studies, 1981

British Library Cataloguing in Publication Data

Pollard, Sidney,
 The integration of the European economy since
 1815. − (Studies on contemporary Europe; No.4).
 1. Europe − Economic integration − History
 I. Title   II. University Association of
 Contemporary European Studies   III. Series
 337.1′4   HC241   80−41914

 ISBN 0−04−336069−6
 ISBN 0−04−336070−X Pbk

Satellite picture of Europe reproduced courtesy of the Commission of the European Communities

Set in 11 on 13 point Plantin by Computacomp (UK) Ltd., Fort William, Scotland
and printed in Great Britain by Billing and Sons Ltd., Guildford, London and Worcester

Contents

Editor's Preface

The University Association for Contemporary European Studies (UACES) exists to promote the study of contemporary European society in all its aspects. To do so it brings together a large number of scholars from many different disciplines. One motivating force for these scholars has been an awareness of the inadequacy of their particular scholarly discipline to provide satisfactory answers to the complex problems which they were handling both in research and in teaching. Many aspects of contemporary European economy, society and politics are indeed hard to illuminate if the light comes from only one of the traditional disciplines of academic study and this has meant that teachers, students and everybody else are frequently without adequate information on topics of immediate and important interest. The Association has therefore commissioned scholars currently working in such areas to present in short form studies of problems which are of special importance, or specially noteworthy because of the lack of easily accessible information about them in current public and academic discussion. The studies are written by experts in each particular topic. They are not, however, merely for teachers and students, but for anyone who may wish to find out something further about subjects which are now much discussed but about which real information is still hard to come by. In this way the Association hopes it may bring closer what are often the separate worlds of academic and public knowledge while at the same time providing a service to readers and students in a relatively new field of study.

ALAN S. MILWARD
University of Manchester Institute of Science and Technology

I *Introduction*

Nowadays 'economic integration' is one of the most frequently used phrases in current affairs, in Europe and elsewhere. Passions are roused for and against it, and a great many political institutions have been modified to accommodate it including the very concept of national sovereignty, which at one time was the one fixed pole in a shifting world of political definitions. Many, perhaps most, who are concerned with it believe that it has an important historical dimension: if they favour it, they see it as the outcome of a long common heritage in Europe; and similarly those who oppose its further progress do so mostly because they feel that it will destroy the historical independence of their country or their nation. This book sets out to examine some of the historical background to the current drive to economic integration as applied to Europe.

Perhaps the first thing of interest to notice is how comparatively new the term itself is in this context. In its negative form, as 'disintegration', it appeared in the late 1930s to describe what had happened to the European and the world economy: the positive form surfaced in the English-speaking world only in 1947–8. The absence of a word and its equivalents generally means that the concept itself was not in frequent use; but now that it has passed into common parlance there is no agreement as to its precise meaning. It is clear that it must mean more than the traditional customs union, under which member countries enjoyed complete freedom of trade within while maintaining a unified tariff to trade without. In modern conditions any approach to fair competition within such a customs union must include at least some alignment of taxation, of social welfare schemes, of subsidies, postal services, and the like. Moreover, free trade in commodities would constitute a very limited form of liberalisation without freedom of movement for capital and labour as well. But there is no agreement as to how to evaluate these different aspects of economic integration or which of them to consider vital and which subsidiary. We cannot even agree, in comparing two systems having integrated different facets of the economy, along different routes of approach, which would be the more 'integrated': the rough and ready measure of the proportion of trade to national income often conceals more than it reveals. In any case, it can be shown that the desirable aim is not the maximum, but the optimum, of centralisation (Tinbergen, 1965, p. 21).

When there are problems of definition it is often useful to fall back on historical context. Here we see basically two lines of advance that have led, in turn, to two types of support for European economic integration, though they are not mutually exclusive.

The first centres on a 'natural' economic process, not necessarily planned or willed by anyone, but the outcome of untold separate decisions, each arrived at for reasons of self-interest without ulterior political motives. In economies in which decisions are decentralised in this way, such as have become typical for Europe in recent centuries, the tendency would be for methods that were technologically superior in a cost-effective sense to drive out those that were inferior. The power of competitive superiority was strong enough to force also organisations and social structures to adapt themselves to these technological innovations. Thus as machines proved superior to hand methods and drove people using hand methods out of business, and as machines could be used effectively only in factories, factories were adopted as workplaces. Again, as railways were more efficient than earlier forms of transport and railways needed vast concentrations of capital, new methods were found to collect, control and sometimes guarantee the interest on such large sums. But further, as railways became more efficient still if they could cover the whole continent rather than stop at frontiers, their own internal logic forced the countries of Europe to give up some of their own decision-making power in order to obtain things the railways required, such as a common gauge, timetable alignments, or through traffic agreements. Thus the logic of much of the new technology, in transport and in communications, but also in mass production, in the exchange of scientific information and in many other spheres, imposed a growing degree of integration on the European economy.

A second line of advance started at the political, if not idealistic plane. The idealised concept of a European continent sharing a common Christian cultural heritage has existed since the Middle Ages, and it has led to repeated calls for a Europe unified also in the political sense, for the opening of the frontiers and the brotherhood of European man. There has scarcely been an age without some such manifesto, whether under the aegis of the Christian religion or under the banner of the common humanity of the Enlightenment, but it seems clear that the frequency and the power of such calls increased in the later eighteenth and the nineteenth centuries. It was then that some of the most advanced spirits of the age, like the Abbé de Saint-Pierre, Jean-Jacques Rousseau and Jeremy Bentham, advocated a European senate or parliament and even a

European army to set the seal on the political unification of the continent, and they were followed by many lesser lights. Their hopes would naturally include the unification of economic policy-making for the benefit of the whole of Europe.

Different though these two approaches are, they have one thing in common: in both economic integration was not the aim of policy as such, but was to emerge as a by-product of other developments, in one case as a by-product of technical and economic progress, and in the other as a by-product of political unification. This, we shall find, is an essential part of the history of the move to economic integration even after 1815 and to the present: it is, with few exceptions, not the history of a conscious and purposeful movement, but of the emergence of a concept, in theory and even in practice, while the human actors, the great and the powerful, were pursuing other interests. Economic integration was rarely the subject of world-shaking dedication and enthusiasm, of political oratory or personal self-sacrifice, but rather the result of slow, piecemeal and unspectacular progress. To some extent it still has that character today. Yet it forms one of the profoundest and most significant developments of the past century and a half.

In its modern connotation, economic integration is understood to have a supranational meaning: it is taken to signify the breakdown of national barriers in order to allow economic links, such as freedom to trade, to migrate and take jobs, and equality of treatment before the law, to exist over two or more countries as if the area were part of a single national community. It therefore appears as the antithesis, as the supersession, of national exclusiveness, of national sovereignty and autarky. Today economic integration signifies the opposite of economic nationalism.

This was not always so. It is possible, following Myrdal's lead (Myrdal, 1956) to understand by economic integration in the first instance the integration of economic life *within* the existing nation states, such as occurred in the major European states in the eighteenth and above all the nineteenth centuries. This refers not merely to the breakdown of internal customs barriers and the free movement of commodities, of which more below; it refers specifically to the creation of greater equality of opportunities and rights of citizenship, which were, in turn, part of the same movement that created the modern bourgeois-liberal nation state itself in Europe.

In some sense, all these were outcomes of improved technology and of economic growth. Only the means which became available after the breakthrough of the British industrial revolution made it both possible and necessary to open up the whole of the large internal markets of the major states, to even out tax payments, to develop national education systems, to unify currency and banking policy and to provide ever more comprehensive rights of citizenship to all citizens within the national borders. In this phase of history, which in the West lasted until about the 1870s or possibly a little beyond, the development of the nation state and of economic integration marched in step, mutually reinforcing each other.

It is only since then that these two great movements of the modern period have become separated, if not totally opposed to each other, so that those who favour the advance towards greater economic integration of Europe have had to take up an anti-nationalist posture, and those who wish to oppose the further progress towards European economic integration find that it is most easily done by beating the nationalist drum. Indeed, in the worst years of economic disintegration, in the years following the Great Depression of the early 1930s, this confrontation between nationalism and integration seemed to be inevitable. The attitudes have survived, but their rigidity is no longer appropriate today.

For in the dialectical way in which much of history seems to proceed, the return to an integrative economic development in

Europe has not taken place, as in the first part of the last century, by transcending or by-passing the nation state, but rather through its own actions and initiative. The hostility between sovereign state and economic integration was never inevitable, but always time-bound; and given the right economic needs and technical opportunities, we are finding now that it is through the actions of the established national governments, pursuing what they conceive to be their own interests, that economic integration is taken forward into a new phase. The following chapters will attempt to describe the process of historical change in its chronological sequence.

2 *1815 – the Last Phase of a Traditional World*

The world which had come to an end with the advances of the revolutionary and later Napoleonic French armies had not been a stable world. On the contrary, one of its most marked characteristics was a growing tension between actual, and even more clearly potential, economic progress and the hampering actions of absolutist, frequently semi-feudal, rulers and governments clinging to traditional economic policies.

The eighteenth century had seen enormous advances in technology, and until its last two decades there were several industrial regions on the continent as advanced and as capable of accepting and perfecting new methods as the leading regions in Britain. The great Encyclopaedia produced in thirty-five volumes by the savants of the French Enlightenment between 1751 and 1780 was full of the new technical marvels used in industry, mining and transport, together with the latest discoveries of pure science, and these entries were frequently being overtaken by further innovations almost as soon as they were printed. More significantly still, large concentrations of domestic workers had begun to form in several regions, making such things as textile and metal goods, clocks, or wooden articles, and there were also to be found, in many parts of

Europe, large and imposing manufactories or workshops, either engaged in finishing the goods produced by these outworkers, or in large-scale production of such items as glassware, arms, pottery and luxury furniture and furnishings. All of these worked for distant markets, in some cases abroad or overseas, and therefore required a complex system of transport, trading and finance to sustain the level of output on which their specialisation depended.

Against this, the means of transport were inefficient, primitive, or non-existent over much of Europe. Overland, laborious carriage by pack animals was the rule since there were very few roads capable of taking wheeled traffic over any distance, while river navigation was limited by shoals, rapids and, above all, by the obstruction of frontiers, staple rights, tolls and costly delays, including at times the needless chicanery of having to tranship goods in transit. Things were worst in Germany, where political power was divided among hundreds of kingdoms, dukedoms, counties, cities, bishoprics and other petty independent sovereignties, their frontiers intermingling in a nightmare of dynastic confusion. In the absence of good roads most long-distance traffic there went by water, yet shipping on the relatively short stretch of the Elbe from Dresden to Magdeburg passed no fewer than sixteen customs houses, while on the Rhine between Duisburg and the Dutch border, not far away, there were thirty tolls to be paid, and a similar number on the Main between Bamberg and Mainz, and on the Weser between Minden and Elsfleth. Altogether there were 1,800 customs frontiers in Germany at the end of the eighteenth century, and even the merchant trying to avoid them and keeping to the main countries found that between Hamburg and Austria, for example, and between Berlin and Switzerland, he had to cross ten customs lines and as many independent administrations.

It may be thought that in these examples traffic and trade

were the victims of political ineptitude, and it was the necessity of the political constitution which enforced all these costs on German producers and consumers. However, it should be stressed that customs were not normally levied at frontiers: these were usually too convoluted, and the population behind them was too small, for that. Instead they were usually collected at the town gates or along roads and rivers, and they were based on privileges, exclusive rights, exemptions and hereditary patents, frequently going back to periods in which economic reality had borne a quite different character. Even Prussia, the largest state, had some sixty different custom and excise rates, and levied them on traffic passing between the different provinces and from the countryside into the cities, as well as at the frontier.

Moreover, things were not very much better in the apparently unitary monarchy of France, the epitome at the time of the centralised state. Fiscally France was administered by the 'Five Great [Tax] Farms' covering much of the northern half of the kingdom around Paris, by a group of provinces 'regarded as foreign' covering much of France south of the Loire as well as French Flanders, Artois and Brittany, and by 'provinces effectively foreign', such as Alsace and the Franche Comté. There were also free ports. Between them there were customs barriers and other obstructions. Similarly, on a river like the Rhône there were twelve tolls to be paid between Châlons and Lyons, and eighteen tolls between Lyons and Arles – though the tolls were low and their nuisance value was greater than the value of the revenue they raised. Nor were conditions much different elsewhere: thus the Habsburg Empire maintained customs frontiers between its individual provinces while the Italian peninsula was carved up among different sovereigns like parts of Germany.

The economic philosophy held ostensibly by the rulers of these territories and of others in Europe was mercantilism. It was a broad philosophy, providing a framework which allowed many variants in detail according to the circumstances of the country concerned. Moreover, it did not stand still but had developed over the centuries. One central assumption, however, was found in all the variants, to the effect that it was the role of the economy to strengthen the power of the state – rather than, as has become central to more recent economic thinking, to maximise the welfare of individuals. Two of the main methods advocated for achieving that aim were a 'positive' balance of trade, ensuring that more gold and currency flowed in than flowed out, and the creation of the largest possible range of industries at home, so as to become independent of foreign suppliers. In the later stages in the eighteenth century exports were to be encouraged and imports discouraged for the additional reason of creating employment at home, and firms and industries asking their governments or rulers for protection came increasingly to do so on the grounds that such a policy would set large numbers of the poor to work, or stave off their unemployment, respectively.

There were various ways of achieving these aims, including the grant of subsidies, privileges and monopolies to certain manufacturers, and the attraction of labour, particularly skilled and managerial labour, from abroad, as well as the prevention of the emigration of skilled workers to rival territories. But the most obvious method was a policy of protection at the frontiers, by means of customs dues and outright prohibitions of imports.

It is evident that there is a strong similarity between the mercantilist range of policies and the policies and arguments put forward by protectionists in more recent times, and indeed modern protectionism is occasionally referred to as neo-mercantilism. Both start from the belief that exports are desirable and imports undesirable, the former to be furthered and subsidised, if need be, the latter to be discouraged and taxed. Both believe in a wide variety of industry at home, rather than in strengthening an international division of labour; and above all, as their central canon, both believe that the objective of policy is to benefit the home country, even if it is at the expense of the foreigner, and that these two interests are opposed to each other. The economic world, like the political, is seen as the battleground of each country against all.

Yet what is most remarkable is that many, perhaps most, of the provisions that we have described as being actually in force and that were designed to limit trade and mutual economic intercourse between states and nations were not at all of a kind to further the mercantilist objectives. To some extent the explanation must be found in the internal contradictions of mercantilism itself. Thus while it was in general in favour of an export surplus and of maximising exports for that reason, it also had a 'provisioning' policy, to *prevent* the export of and keep at home certain strategic goods, like grain, wool, or other raw materials. 'Every nation', said Alexander Hamilton, 'ought to endeavour to possess within itself all the essentials of national supply ... The possession of these is necessary ... to the safety as well as to the welfare of the society' ('Report on manufactures', in *Papers on Public Credit, Commerce and Finance*, 1934 reprint, pp. 227–8). The confusion is in part between the capacity to produce goods, which clearly fits in with mercantilist overall objectives, and the goods themselves: thus the taxing of certain exports, like coal in Britain, would make sense only in supply terms though it ran right against the overall policy of boosting exports. But there were also numerous other measures in existence which cannot be explained in mercantilist terms at all.

If the King of France, for example, wanted to encourage certain industries in his dominions, such as the printing and finishing of cotton *indiennes* in Alsace, why should he levy import duties on these goods and then create other difficulties for them when they entered the central provinces of France?

The German princes also, surely, should have taxed imports at the frontier rather than let them cross all frontiers freely and then charge duties, on both home and foreign products, at the towns' gates? It made surely the reverse of mercantilist sense for the King of Prussia to hamper the export of the products of one of his provinces by levying a duty on them as they entered another.

There was indeed a contradiction there, and it is, in principle, the contradiction between our present notion of the desirability, or even the inevitability, of expansion, and the mercantilist's notion of a static world, in which the only chance of progress was to achieve it at the expense of someone else.

'Commerce', declared Colbert, the greatest of them all, in 1669, 'is carried on by 20,000 vessels and that number cannot be increased. Each nation strives to have its fair share and to get ahead of the others ... [England and France] can improve their commerce only by increasing the number of their vessels and can increase this number only ... by paring away from the 15,000 to 16,000 Dutch ships.' (*Lettres, instructions, mémoires*, Paris, 1861–70, Vol. VI, p. 269)

In such a world defence is better than change and expansion, economic efficiency as such has subordinate significance, and the raising of taxes and revenues for the ruler is as always more important than the free flow of innovating trade. Moreover, it is clear that in such a world trade itself plays only a marginal role in economic life, affecting surpluses and luxuries rather than essentials, for if trade had been essential it would have forced a channel for itself. In the same way, poor roads and harbours reflect a low level of traffic as well as being a hindrance to it, for heavy traffic soon creates its own routes. When the innovations occurred the men who produced them, the manufacturers and traders, and particularly those who did not enjoy royal favours or monopolies, could not be expected to accept these restrictions and obstructions. The resulting tensions mounted everywhere, and exploded in the French revolution.

The French Third Estate left no doubt as to where their preferences lay. Within the very first months of their seizure of power all laws forbidding the circulation of goods had been annulled (1789) and so had all seigneurial tolls with the ending of 'feudalism'. In 1790 all internal customs duties were abolished and switched to the frontiers, and a commission to unify weights and measures was appointed to deal with another source of friction and obstruction under the *ancien régime*. In the following year all privileged companies, guilds and inspectors of industry, together with the regulations they administered, were abolished, and trade unions prohibited. At the same time a new protective tariff was imposed (and justified in the name of 'freedom'), export taxes on French goods going to the colonies were repealed and all foreigners were excluded from trade with the French colonies. In 1793 all colonial duties were repealed, a Navigation Act was passed, and the use of British manufactures was prohibited, including those already in the country. The next few years saw increases in tariff levels and further measures against British manufactures and, on the positive side, the creation of a unified system of weights, measures and currency, and a code of laws favouring trade, industry and the sanctity of commercial contracts.

Among the turmoils of war and revolution the French were thus completing the economic integration of their country at unprecedented speed. At the same time they were trying to protect it against foreign competition in industry, trade and shipping: a dual aim with which we have become very familiar since.

The claim was made, then and later, and even by Napoleon himself musing in exile on St Helena, that as the revolution spread outward and as the French conquered one country after another, they were launched on a path of extending that integration to the whole of Europe by unifying its economy, the first stage being the continental system by which Napoleon waged an economic war against Britain from 1806 onward. The attempt, it is sometimes said, failed only because of the collapse of Napoleon's empire.

Nothing could be further from the truth. It was indeed the French strategy to close the continent as a whole to British goods and British shipping, in the same way that the British were attempting to blockade all ports in enemy hands. But the sole beneficiary of the French policy was to be the (enlarged) French Empire. Other countries on its edge, notably Italy, were to become France's suppliers of certain raw materials and markets for its manufactures. The rest of Europe, in as much as it entered into the picture at all, was to become a dependency, to be flooded by the protected and pampered industries of France while the manufactures produced there were wholly excluded from the metropolitan market. The French vision was that of an exclusive nationalism.

After total defeat in 1815 nothing remained of France's political dreams, but the clock could not be turned back in economic and social matters. The roads, the river improvements, the abolition of feudal and seigneurial obstructions, the commercial code, the new weights and measures remained wherever they had penetrated, acting also as an example to the rest where they had not.

Beyond all this, however, the French wars had left one yet more portentous heritage for the future. It derived from the growing isolation of the continent in twenty-two years of war from the new technology which was then developing at great speed in Britain, particularly in the textile and iron industries and in engineering. Normally contact with other manufacturing countries would have been sufficiently close to allow them either to copy, or to learn to protect themselves against, the more advanced or the cheaper British imports as they developed stage by stage. As it was, when the shipping lanes and ports were once more opened after the war a flood of British products burst over the unprepared markets. Their prices were exceptionally low because of the postwar crisis in which British markets at home and abroad collapsed, leading to widespread bankruptcies. Many of the most promising firms on the continent, and indeed whole industrial regions, went under in this flood. They were unable to sell their products and their workers were thrown out of work by the thousand by what they considered dumped goods from Britain. It took many years, and in some cases decades, to rebuild the promising industrial beginnings destroyed then.

The circumstances were quite exceptional, but the experience was traumatic. A whole generation of manufacturers, merchants and economic advisers grew up for whom freedom of trade meant inevitable defeat and destruction at the hands of the British competition based on superior technology, and who were therefore wedded to protectionist beliefs in the interests of their own countries. The most eloquent of them was the German-American Friedrich List, who considered that free trade might be advisable as between equals, but that in view of the lead gained by the British any country that wished to build up its own industries had to have a protective wall in order to keep out British goods until its own industries had reached a similar level of efficiency. The free trade sentiments which began to emanate from Britain were for similar reasons treated with suspicion all over the continent, and not without cause, as a doctrine which would favour the British export industries as against all others.

Europe in consequence split into two groups. The large countries with reasonably strong central administrations that could hope to nurture a varied assortment of industry within their own borders, above all France, became strongly protectionist, imposing high tariffs or total prohibitions on manufactured and other imports. The countries that were too small to rely on home markets and that had to have exports in order to provide large enough sales for their industries as well as those too small to guard their frontiers, and those, like the northern provinces of the Netherlands and the German free cities of Hamburg, Bremen and Frankfurt/Main, which lived by trading rather than producing, held to free trade or moderate duties and favoured close economic relations between states.

The results were mixed, and clearly depended on many factors other than the commercial policies pursued. There were some industrial centres, like the Belgian coalfield, that developed extremely successfully within a largely protectionist environment; but on the whole it was areas with little or no protection and with liberal policies, such as Switzerland, Rhineland-Westphalia and Saxony, that made the most progress. By contrast, the countries with the most rigid protection of their frontiers, including Spain, Austria, Russia and to some extent even France, showed very little progress, except near the frontier, as in northern Bohemia or Alsace, where smuggling may have not been without significance.

3 Industrialisation and the Progressive Economic Integration of Europe from 1815 to the 1870s

In the years after 1815 both Britain, as the successful industrialiser, and France, whose revolution became an inspiration to reformers everywhere, were taken as models in many parts of Europe. The concept of 'progress' came to mean the imitation and catching up of one or other or both of them, and among the barriers to that progress that were becoming increasingly oppressive were the barriers to the trade in goods and the movement of people, especially those within countries. The internal economic integration achieved by these two leading countries in Europe, as well as by the United States of America, became a desirable objective in the pursuit of which both nationalists and those hoping for economic progress could unite. It was their hope that Europe would become a continent of large integrated free-trade areas.

The first and most successful drive in that direction arose in Germany. It ultimately led to the formation of the Zollverein, or German Customs Union. Its initial impetus came not from any urge to institute freer trade within the country, though it had been agreed on the reconstitution of the German Confederation in 1815 that the various states should take an early opportunity to ease trade and speed the flow of river traffic

27

between them; still less was the Zollverein intended to be the first step towards the political unification of Germany under Prussian leadership, as some later historians implied. Instead it derived from the attempts within the Prussian civil service to make the state apparatus more efficient and more modern as part of the belated reactions to the humiliation of Prussia by the French in the war. It was the hope to collect more taxes at lower cost and with less damage to trade that induced Prussia in 1816–18 to abolish the internal excise and tariff duties and instead levy a simplified tariff on imports from abroad.

The new system of tax collection, besides being more efficient, was also more liberal. It was certainly the most liberal in any major country in Europe at the time. Under the new law, all prohibitions on imports were ended and all import duties on raw materials abolished; tariffs on manufactures were kept low and only tropical goods and a few other items carried a high tariff for revenue purposes. On the other hand, transit dues, paid largely by the citizens of the smaller German states, were pitched at a high level. Overall, it was a system of low rates in part because Prussia could not afford to antagonise its more powerful neighbours and feared retaliation if it set them too high, but also because the manufacturing interests were still weak in the eastern and politically dominant part of the kingdom. The ruling class of landowners was connected with the production of grain, the country's main export commodity, and its natural free trade instincts were supported by the powerful merchant communities of some of the port towns.

The method of collecting all duties at the frontiers undermined the economic independence of those other states which lay wholly or in part in enclaves within Prussian territory, a phenomenon which the simplification of the 1815 constitution had by no means ended. After much friction they were incorporated in the customs territory, receiving part of the sums collected by the Prussian officials at the frontier according to a previously agreed key, based essentially on relative population.

It should be noted that these customs arrangements did not imply political agreement or subordination; on the contrary, so great was the antagonism among some of the customs partners that even as late as 1866 they went to war on the side of Austria and against Prussia, though they continued to remit and receive the appropriate tax payments right through the fighting. In the 1820s, also, the reaction of the other larger states in central and southern Germany was to set up customs unions of their own in order to stand up to Prussia, but this drive for independence was defeated by the economic logic of the benefits to be derived from association with the larger country. One by one, the majority of the other states agreed to enter the Prussian scheme, and on 1 January 1834 eighteen states with a population of over 23 million came together as the Zollverein, forming a single customs territory. Others joined later, and integration was extended into other spheres of the economy also: in particular, the Zollverein currencies were put on a common basis in 1857 and there were common post office facilities. In the course of time Prussia learnt to tie the other countries to itself politically by some sacrifice in tax revenue, and ultimately to use the economic hold it had thus acquired over its partners to prevent Austria, the other major German state, from taking over the leadership in a united Germany. Meanwhile, a large free internal market to rival those of France and Britain had been created, and it led directly to the formation of the German Empire in 1871.

Germany thus became for a time a shining example of the moving power of the logic of economic integration, as well as of the possibility of shaping a large internal free trade area out of separate units. How far that success depended on the strongly nationalist centripetal forces in Germany as well as on the remarkably successful industrialisation drive which occurred at the same time it is not easy to establish, nor can we be certain to what extent the existence of the Zollverein had helped forward that process of industrialisation itself. The German industrial revolution rested substantially on the key heavy industries of the Ruhr and of Upper Silesia, and the engineering industries of Berlin and their development, in turn, owed a great deal to the railways which must be given a considerable share of the credit for both the economic unification and the speedy industrialisation of the country.

Others followed a similar path. The Austrian provinces of the Habsburg Empire had been formed into a customs union with Bohemia in 1775. In 1849 the Italian provinces of Parma and Modena were brought in, and Hungary with Croatia, Slavonia and Transylvania in 1850 and 1851. Moldavia and Wallachia formed a customs union in 1847, Russia with Poland in 1850, the Swiss cantons in 1848, and Italy was unified economically as well as politically in 1860–6. The political circumstances no less than the stages of economic progress reached in these territories showed wide differences, but it is clear that their moves attempted to capture some of the advantages derived by the leading countries from their internal economic integration.

There were several concrete proposals that failed to materialise, quite a number of them because of the jealousy of outside powers who were left out and feared for their established favoured positions. These include the proposed Franco-Belgian union of 1835–42, and the Dutch-Belgian union proposals of 1878 and 1907. The attempts by Austria to break into the charmed circle of the German Zollverein, pursued with some vigour in 1849–53, ultimately foundered on the refusal of Prussia to tolerate a more powerful rival within the union, as well as on the high tariff walls maintained by Austria which were quite incompatible with the standards of the others.

Customs unions were not the only expressions of a drawing together of economic Europe. A common currency has in recent years been seen to be one of the key factors determining the convergence or divergence of economic policy. The most interesting of the nineteenth-century attempts to unify currency across political frontiers was the Latin Monetary Union. It was based on the French system, rigidly bimetallic since 1803, to which, in spite of its instability, the Belgian franc had been aligned in 1832, the Swiss franc in 1850 and the Italian currency in 1862. These might be seen as the outcome of a natural evolution, but in times of stress governments did not hesitate to snatch temporary advantages from competitive depreciation by reducing the fineness of their coinage, while holding to the agreed standard weights. A conference in 1865 ultimately settled fineness as well as weight, and the group was later joined by Greece (1867), while others like Spain and Romania also aligned their currency with the Latin system. The Northern Monetary Union of Sweden, Norway and Denmark was formally established in 1873.

Both these were overshadowed in significance by the gold standard of the pound sterling, centred on London but embracing most of the British Empire as well as many overseas countries dependent on European markets. Sterling's fixed parity with gold ensured a common base with every other currency also tied to gold, such as the US dollar. Germany went over to gold in 1873 and gradually an effective unitary system, held together in practice by the open economy of Britain in which gold and all other commodities entering international trade could be sold freely, was established in the years to 1914. The gold standard created strong links within the whole of the civilised world which even such troubled economies as the Austrian or the Russian made considerable sacrifices to join.

Yet it was commodity trade that was believed to represent most clearly the principle of integration within the European economy. It was freed gradually from the obstruction inherited from earlier centuries and strengthened further after the experience of 1815–17. The middle of the nineteenth century marked the high peak of the free trade era.

The first moves, among the larger countries at least, were made by Britain. After some tentative easing of tariffs, the main changes occurred in the 1840s with the repeal of the Corn Laws in 1846 and the ending of the Navigation Acts (1849), as well as the ending of the prohibition on exports of machinery. By 1860 practically all protective duties had been removed, and revenue duties only remained. This was accompanied by a widely, though by no means universally, held philosophy sometimes known as 'Manchesterism' according to which growing economic interdependence would not only make the nations of Europe richer and develop their full economic potential, but would also make major wars between them impossible.

Arising from a country which was then at the height of its technical advantage over all others, the undisputed 'workshop of the world', such views, even when accompanied by the action of freeing all imports from taxes and restrictions, might be suspect, and many on the continent held them to be so. The British vision of forming the manufacturing centre in Europe to which all others supplied raw materials and food, while taking their industrial goods from Britain and thus inhibiting the development of their own industries, was too close to reality to be comfortable to the others who had ambitions to reap the advantages of modern industry themselves. Nevertheless, those years saw a significant if gradual penetration of free-trade policies in practice into much of the advanced world of the day.

The main instrument was the trade treaty, accompanied by substantial reductions in tariffs between the partners and a 'most favoured nation' clause under which any treaty partner was entitled to any additional reductions in tariffs made to third countries. As long as these treaties lasted the trend in protection could thus only be downwards, and any concession made to one opened the way to further concessions to others.

The first such treaty was concluded between Britain and France in 1860. Sometimes known as the 'Cobden–Chevalier' Treaty after its chief negotiators, it followed some years of gradual liberalisation both in Britain under Gladstone and in France under Napoleon III. Britain, being practically a free-trade nation at the time, had fewer concessions to offer than France, which agreed to end all prohibitions and to reduce all tariff rates to a maximum of 30 per cent in two years and a maximum of 25 per cent in five years; in practice, most rates were reduced to well below these levels. There was a clear risk in these concessions to certain French industries which had grown up behind a high tariff shelter, particularly the iron-making and textile branches, and they were aided by temporary state loans on easy terms; other French industries, like silks, fashion goods and wine, benefited at once. Nevertheless, the tariff was unpopular among the ruling middle classes in France, and it would not have been passed if it had required parliamentary sanction.

France now had two tariffs, a low-level one for Britain, and a high-level one for everyone else. This forced others to seek to obtain similar concessions in order to keep a foothold in the French market, and there were soon numerous negotiations in progress with that objective in mind. One of the earliest results was the Delbrück–Le Clerq agreement on mutual tariff reductions between Prussia and France. Several of the other members of the Zollverein were unhappy with that change and had a right of veto, but Prussia made acceptance of the treaty a condition of her own renewal of her Zollverein membership in 1865, and such was her ascendancy at the time that the treaty was ultimately accepted by all the other members. Other countries with which France concluded similar treaties were

33

Belgium (1862), Italy (1863), Switzerland (1864), Sweden-Norway, the Hanse towns, Spain and Holland (1865), Austria (1866) and Portugal (1867). Each of these others made treaties with other major trading partners in turn in those years, and the result was a comprehensive network of trading agreements which ensured a low and declining level of protection and therefore a growing degree of economic interconnection between countries.

A liberal phase in the economic development of Europe had begun. Unlike some earlier examples of freedom from frontier control, it was not based on the technical inability to levy duties or on the insignificant quantity of the traffic, but on the conscious decisions of modern governments to encourage the closer integration of European economic life by opening out the opportunities of international trade and competition. There were mixed motives in every country, and mixed reactions, ranging from enthusiasm to bitter opposition. Export industries and export sectors everywhere favoured the freeing of trade, and previously sheltered sectors fearing import competition were everywhere opposed to it; but the fact that Britain and the other leading countries were flourishing under freer trade, while the most backward countries, like Russia, maintained their rigid systems of prohibitions and protection, weighed with all shades of opinion. To contemporaries who, like people in all ages, tended to believe that all preceding history represented a slow upward climb to their own unprecedentedly high level of civilisation, it seemed as though the benighted and restrictive ages of darkness of the past were giving way to the shining light of progress which included the orthodox doctrines of free-trade economists, and protectionists were very much on the defensive, having to rely on sectional and selfish special pleading. None of them knew how short that liberal interlude would turn out to be.

Over much of the nineteenth century the debate between

protectionists and free traders was the most hotly contested issue of economic policy, and the dispute has by no means been settled even today, though it has lost its front rank. In the enormous literature which developed on the subject there is a similar divergence of views to this day on how far this liberal interlude succeeded in fostering or inhibiting economic growth and prosperity. It is not too difficult, by choosing one's examples carefully enough, to make out a case for the view that these years showed unprecedented economic growth and development in Europe, that previously sluggish and inefficient industries were stimulated into modernisation, that the heavy capital investment especially in railways, engineering and heavy industries, on which the future progress of Europe depended was called forth by the expansion of international trade which resulted from the liberalisation, and that without it the continental economies would have remained more backward and their people the poorer. Similarly, by selecting different data, it can be shown that free trade killed off numerous old-established industries, causing widespread social problems, that such growth as was achieved led to overspeculation, crises and depression in the 1870s, and – a point with very strong appeal to twentieth-century economists – that growth rates accelerated everywhere, except in Great Britain which alone had benefited from liberalism and therefore stuck to it, as soon as protection for home industries was reintroduced in the 1870s and 1880s.

Both theory and experience have taken long strides forward since those decades and, in common with the most advanced contemporary thinkers, economists today would not be dogmatic on the effects of protection or free trade in general, but would relate them to the stage of economic development reached as well as to other specific circumstances of the economies concerned. Most countries were then about to, or hoping to, industrialise on the British model, but were having to do it in the shadow of British competition as well as of the competition of other near neighbours. The 'infant industry' argument of the day, still widely held to be valid, would assert that that was precisely the stage at which rigid protection was called for, to give the new industries a chance to develop until they were strong enough to stand up to the more experienced foreign rivals. The industrial revolution, for such as List and his followers, was precisely the time when protection should be high, even if one were to favour free trade before and after that phase.

Yet it cannot be denied that such countries as France, Belgium and Germany took some giant strides in the industrialisation of their main regions precisely in this phase of freer trade, the German states, indeed, having had only a low though varying level of protection for most key manufactures for the whole of the period since 1833. The mechanism by which this occurred has often been misunderstood, largely because it depended on the relatively long timespans involved, while most economic theory assumes induced changes to be instantaneous.

In that phase of nineteenth-century European economic history a relatively backward country trading with a technologically more advanced country would find that the latter was not equally advanced in all sectors, but in many industries still used a technology no different from the traditional methods in use everywhere else. At the same time it paid higher wages because of its generally higher level of productivity, and it paid these higher wages even in the sectors in which it had no, or only a very small, technological lead. This gave the more backward country its chance. For while it would be unable to compete even in its own home market against imports from the advanced country produced by the most advanced technical mass-production means, since by definition it was not yet capable of copying those means, it would hold its own, not only at home, but even abroad and perhaps even in the advanced country itself, in those commodities in which its technology was not inferior and in which therefore its lower real wage level gave it lower prices.

In the same way the less developed country, say, Prussia or Baden in 1815–70, would have even less developed trading partners to whom, in turn, it might appear as the technically more advanced economy, using more efficient methods in some sectors but paying higher wages in all. The same trading pattern would therefore emerge at, as it were, a lower level of technology and of wages. Typically, what would be sent outwards from the most advanced technological centres, formed by Britain at first, but also Belgium, Switzerland and parts of France and Germany later, would be mass-produced semi-manufactures, like textile yarn and pig iron; what would come back would be finished goods, like woven fabrics or iron ware. Similarly, what went out lower down the 'gradient' of technology in Europe would be manufactured finished goods, and what came back would be products depending entirely on handicraft unaided by machinery. In addition, and ultimately of critical importance, the most advanced centres would export machinery and technological know-how, and from below would come primary and agricultural products all the way up the line. All this was, of course, superimposed on a traditional and surviving trade of exchanging natural resources that simply were not available in the right quantities elsewhere, such as furs from Russia, iron ore from Sweden, or coal from Great Britain.

Two points should be stressed about that trading pattern as it came to dominate Europe in this period. The first is that it constituted a single network, covering Europe as a whole, in which each part was vitally meshed in with every other. The equally vital links between it and the rest of the globe, particularly North America, the temperate zone regions of recent settlement and the tropical and subtropical regions, were at the same time becoming more significant, though they cannot be considered further here. Within Europe, the economic development of, say, Britain, cannot be explained except by taking the role of the country in the total framework of European development into account, and the same is true for the history of, say, Prussia as a country of the intermediate ring, or of Russia or Spain in the outer periphery of development.

The second point to stress is that this is a dynamic picture. It was dynamic in the geographical sense in that the boundaries of areas of 'advanced' technology shifted constantly outwards, raising the status of each new area incorporated, and pushing what was truly peripheral farther and farther away. But it was also dynamic in a truly economic sense, since the very fact of this trade brought machinery to firms in ever new areas; allowing them to use it on the basis of cheapened semi-manufactures, it trained their workers and managers in the uses of new technology and their salesmen in the requirements of foreign countries, and raised skills and expectations everywhere. It was by its nature unstable and progressive, and thus capable of driving the whole of Europe through a particular phase of economic development.

It does not follow that free trade would necessarily show equally positive results in other times and other places, but for Europe in its industrialising phase the free economic intercourse between the regions at different stages of development (quite apart from the benefits of intercourse between regions of different endowment in raw materials, soil, climate, etc.), far from being harmful as so often alleged, was vital for ensuring a fast and healthy development. Tariff walls or prohibitions would have kept from the catching-up nations both the new machinery and technology and the cheap semi-finished goods on which their own progress depended. Europe's industrialisation proceeded relatively smoothly, among other reasons, precisely because it took place within what was in many essentials a single integrated economy, with a fair amount of freedom of movement for labour, a greater amount of freedom for the movement of goods, and the greatest freedom of all for the movement of technology, know-how and capital.

There was thus a certain internal economic logic in the favourable attitude of the major European governments towards greater economic integration, and it was supported also by the logic of much of the new technology itself. This was very clearly so in the case of the new means of transport and communication, and above all in the case of the most far-reaching innovation of all, the railways.

Railways were extremely costly to build by the then current standards of capital accumulation, and the earliest lines everywhere were short, catering for one specific sort of traffic only, like coal, or passengers from the capital city to an upper-class suburb. Nevertheless, such was the internal pressure generated from within a system in which usefulness and profitability were multiplied as it covered greater distances and became part of an ever enlarged network, that all barriers were broken to create huge capital accumulations such as the world had never seen before, with budgets larger than those of many independent states. Railways also crossed frontiers for the same commonsense reasons, though they were thwarted at times by the plans of many governments to build lines essentially for strategic purposes, or for the benefit of the home country only, or, as in the extreme case of Prussia which laid a line for long stretches along the Saxon border without crossing it, to use it to crush once and for all a major industrial and trading rival.

The same logic also applied to rivers, where increasing quantities of traffic could be carried by means of steamboats. Thus on the Rhine complete freedom of navigation to the sea was ensured at last in 1831 and tolls were ended by international agreement on the Scheldt in 1863 and on the

Rhine in 1868. On the Danube the principle of freedom of international navigation was confirmed in 1856, and regulations for traffic were agreed to in 1857 and 1883. On the Elbe traffic rules were eased in 1821 and liberalised in 1861 and 1863, and all tolls were abolished in 1878. The Po, at that time an international river, was freed from tolls by agreement in 1849, confirmed in 1859. Meanwhile Denmark accepted a capital payment of £3·6 million from European trading nations, plus $393,000 from the USA, to end her tolls on passage through the Sound.

Communications had a similar logic. The General (later Universal) Postal Union was established at a conference in Berne in 1874 after earlier regional and bilateral agreements. The telegraph achieved its regulation by the International Telegraph Union in 1865. These, and similar agreements, created international vested interests of their own, in addition to furthering economic integration by the easier movements of men, goods and information.

But beyond it we must not forget the influence of idealism also. Poets, philosophers and sometimes even politicians cherished the notions of a united Europe, or at least a federation that would ensure peace between the nations. In 1814 Henri de Saint-Simon published his plea 'to bring the peoples of Europe into a single body politic while preserving the national independence of each of them'. At the Third International Peace Congress held in Paris in 1849 and attended mostly by delegates from Western countries, Victor Hugo went beyond that federal solution to call for European unity. Following the German Peace Congress of 1867 there appeared a journal called *The United States of Europe* and this was a phrase which enjoyed great popularity from time to time. The actual proposals of these dreamers would, as a matter of course, include sustained economic co-operation, if not total integration within the European economy.

How far these moves might influence the actual treaties made by politicians and the decisions of businessmen it is difficult to say. Clearly the measures of the 1860s and the early 1870s which shaped the liberal interlude in Europe were aided by being launched in an atmosphere of a belief in a common destiny and perhaps even a common brotherhood, though such nebulous notions could never become a major driving force. Altogether, the economic liberalism helped to round off the character of a period in European history when the rise of the nation state and the rise of middle-class power, when technology, economics, the logic of the new means of transport and communication and the imagination of the idealists, all combined to bring the economic integration of Europe one giant step forward.

4

The Conflict between the Economic Urge towards Integration and the Political Drive towards Autarky from the 1870s to 1914

More than two decades of expansion over much of Europe culminated in a great investment boom in 1870–3: factories and railways were built, city development occurred in unprecedented volume, and between them they mopped up all available savings and more. The inevitable collapse which followed ushered in two decades of depression, sometimes known as the 'Great Depression' of the nineteenth century. It is nowadays often remarked that that term is inappropriate in many respects, since the period saw an extremely rapid rise in output, based on the heavy investment of the preceding years; contemporaries, however, felt it to be a disappointing time because of low profits, widespread bankruptcies and widespread unemployment.

Two aspects in particular stood out. One was the fall in prices, which meant that even progressive firms found that their lowering of real costs and increases in output brought no higher profits. The other was the mass influx of grain, mainly from North America and India, made possible by the dramatic reduction in transport costs owing to railway and steamship developments, and helped along by a series of bad harvests in Europe. The effects of these grain imports on the European economy as a whole were profound : within the more advanced countries they threatened the very existence of the agrarian sector by low prices with which European farmers could not compete; in the less advanced areas, the traditional suppliers of food, including Russia, the Danube basin and the Mediterranean countries, they induced a large expansion in output of primary products to make up for the fall in prices, constituting a diversion of resources that might otherwise have been used to build up an infrastructure and more modern methods in industry, and thus keeping the countries poor. The USA, while greatly expanding its grain exports, was also industrialising rapidly and building up its own manufacturing industries, and therefore no longer found it necessary to increase its imports of manufactures in line with its exports to Europe; the resulting unbalance of trade tended to have a depressing effect in Europe not unlike the depressing effects created by the European deficit with the oil producers in the 1970s.

Both industrialists and agrarians felt these developments to be a great disappointment after the promises of the earlier boom years, and they were looking for scapegoats. For once, though for entirely different reasons, they found themselves in agreement in blaming free trade for their troubles, since it had allowed in cheap imports, and it was not difficult to build up an alliance for reintroducing protection in one country after another on that basis.

Yet the protectionists did not have it all their own way. There were in each country those whose specific interests demanded the maintenance of easy movement across frontiers, especially the successful manufacturers for export, those who used cheap imported semi-manufactures, and the traders and financiers. There were also those, led by the orthodox economists, who held to the advantages of free trade on general grounds, as promoting progress and prosperity for all. The wide-ranging debate on this issue, which ultimately even reached the fount and origin of free trade doctrine, Britain itself, showed that quite apart from the sectional vested interests, each of which pretended to speak for the economy as a whole, there was behind the debate a more fundamental conflict of political philosophy and overall view of the role of the state and the nature of the good life. This is particularly evident in the classic debates which took place from the 1890s onward and continued right until the outbreak of the war both in Germany and in Britain.

The German debate is frequently described as the dispute of 'Agrarstaat' versus 'Industriestaat'; that is to say, it was not so much about the methods of regulating trade as about the kind of society in which people wished to live. The protagonists of the industrial economy pointed to the competitive success of German manufacturing which had led to unprecedented rates of expansion in output and employment as well as in exports, making Germany a powerful as well as an increasingly prosperous nation. Its role, like that of Britain before, was to be the producer of engineering and other manufactured products, importing food and raw materials, and increasingly specialising in that role within the European and world economy. Economic growth and industrial power were to be beneficial to both the individual and the state. By contrast, it was argued, the drive to autarky, especially in food, would lead to the emigration of men and of capital, and taxes on food would fall mostly on the poor.

Against this, the supporters of the agrarian economy, whose special interests as agrarians were generally only too obvious, stressed the values of a balanced economy, and the social benefits of a strong, healthy rural farm population, compared with the physically weak, overcrowded, politically radical masses in the industrial towns. They also emphasised the value of being self-sufficient in food in case of war, although as a matter of fact Germany had long since passed the stage at which she could have been made independent of food imports at existing technology. There was also the further rather interesting belief that the heavy dependence on foreign trade was a passing phase, fitting the time when countries were in the process of industrialisation. Once they had all reached a similar level of balanced growth, much of the need for international trade would disappear, and the deliberate drive to autarky would accelerate that process. This school of thought therefore also developed a theorem of the diminishing share of foreign trade in national income as countries advanced in prosperity.

The agrarian protectionists, therefore, far from adapting to a vista of peace, visualised war. They preferred the intangible and possibly mythical 'values' of rural living and attachment to the soil to the more tangible returns in higher incomes, and they clearly preferred rigid conservatism to the dangers of economic and social change. It was a view of the future of their country and of Europe that far transcended the mere economic sphere.

In Britain, too, the protectionist argument had wider implication. The hope of self-supply of food from within the British shores had become utterly unrealistic by the 1890s when this debate was rejoined, but under Joseph Chamberlain the ideal to which the protectionists looked was a self-sufficient empire, in which the mother country would supply the manufactures and the colonies and dominions would provide cheaply produced foodstuffs and the other necessary primary products. This imperialist aim, which depended at least to some extent on the cheap labour in the colonies, was married somewhat incongruously to the argument that tariffs were necessary to protect the British worker from the products of underpaid and sweated foreign labour, and from unemployment arising from foreign imports. In contrast with the German, British protectionism had therefore a strong radical-progressive base, and it was concerned almost exclusively with industrial rather than agrarian protection. But its imperialist implications also had militarist undertones.

Meanwhile, and right through these debates, the economic and technological imperatives which had helped to bring about ever greater economic integration between the countries of Europe continued to operate with increasing power. The spread of industrialisation itself began to change the nature of international trade. Whereas earlier trade had exchanged luxuries, or goods which for reasons of natural endowment could be produced in some areas but not in others, and whereas the industrialisation period itself had developed a third type of international exchange, based on differences in technological progress, now the age that was dawning, in which major trading partners all had developed industry within their borders, was to see the rise of a fourth type of trade, sometimes called a more 'refined' exchange of goods. Here we do not simply find one country exporting, say, textiles to the other, and getting, say, wines in return, but we may find both exporting textile goods to each other, but of different quality, type and design. That is to say, specialisation occurred within finer definitions of 'commodities'. It was a sign both of greater international specialisation and division of labour, and of higher standards of living spreading to larger groups of the population. This effect was to become much more pronounced from the middle of the twentieth century onwards; it was to be the main cause why the prediction of a declining share of foreign trade with economic growth was falsified largely by increasing trade within the advanced countries themselves.

Given growing incomes per head of a growing European population, and trade growing faster than income, international trade and traffic formed one of the fastest growing sectors of the European economy, and the means of transport as well as of communication were among the most spectacular aspects of that growth. By 1870 the enormous network of 65,000 miles of railways had been built in Europe; by 1900 this had expanded almost threefold to 176,000 miles and was still growing. In the later years new building was particularly prominent in the less advanced regions like Russia. There the railways linked raw material and food supplies, such as timber and wheat, with world markets for the first time, making hitherto largely isolated communities into integral parts of the European economy. Docks, harbours and ship canals to take ever larger and more efficient vessels, and the development of river and canal facilities, particularly on the easy terrain of the north European plain, allowed the cheap transport of even bulky goods out of the Ruhr industrial district, for example, or into Berlin.

A glance at the map will reveal that the layout of these means of transport follows in the main the 'natural' demands of producing and consuming centres and centres of population, but there were signs also of increasing direction and distortion for political and strategic reasons: in the more backward countries, indeed, where railways were built largely at the expense of the state and ahead of economic demand, this was more clearly the case, but it was noticeable elsewhere too. Nor was this limited to international links: internal planning could be affected in similar ways also. The blocking of the German east–west Mittellandkanal in the interest of the eastern landowners is a famous example, but the location of many of the French local railway links also bears eloquent witness to the persuasive power of local politicians over railway logic. These distortions were an ominous foretaste of the increasing subordination of economic benefits to political priorities.

Not only goods moved on these means of transport: people also found travel easier and ever cheaper. The migration of labour was an obvious beneficiary. Whereas previously people had moved in a trickle, or in organised groups on the invitation of a prince or under the wing of some religious or other organisation, the movement of individuals now became a flood. At first much of the migration was directed out of Europe, mainly to North America, but in the last decades before the outbreak of war increasing and substantial numbers also migrated within Europe, within as well as across the frontiers. Thus from 1876 on, when official statistical returns were first made, and until 1913, there was an average annual migration of 42,000 Italians to France, 67,000 to Germany and Austria and 33,000 to Switzerland. Significantly, these were mostly seasonal or temporary workers, who had learnt to treat the foreign country as a legitimate part of their own labour market. Very few of them settled permanently: thus in 1911 the total Italian population in France was only 419,000, and in Germany and Austria, 192,000. Similarly, Germany attracted about 800,000 migrant Polish workers every year in the period before the war, of whom around one half worked in the western manufacturing and mining districts, and the rest in agriculture, mostly in the east; this was part of a typical wave migration, the empty spaces on the eastern agrarian estates having been created by the permanent emigration of the German rural workers from there to Berlin and the Ruhr industries. There were also several hundred thousand Austrian workers as well as Russians, Dutch, Belgians and the Italian workers noted above in Germany in those years. France attracted, beside Italian, also Belgian, Spanish and Polish workers. There were similar movements of profound significance within state boundaries, but across national lines, such as the migration of peripheral Slav workers into Vienna and the industrial region around the city, of Irish into Britain, and of members of various nationalities within the Russian Empire into Moscow and Petersburg. Once more, ominously, there were the beginnings of restriction and control by several governments at the end of the period, but it is likely that the frontiers had never before been so easy to cross.

Capital in those years moved more freely still across Europe. The practice of loans to governments from abroad goes back to the golden age of Amsterdam in the seventeenth century if not before. In the first half of the nineteenth century such loans multiplied as London and Paris, together with Hamburg, Frankfurt/Main, Amsterdam and Basle, became centres of international lending. It was above all the railways which spread these international capital movements into the private sector. Some of the early Belgian and French railways were built by British capital in the 1840s, but it was from the 1850s on that the two rival French groups, the Crédit Mobilier and the Rothschilds, vied for railway contracts and investments abroad, in Austria, Italy, Spain and farther afield. The Russian railways were largely financed from abroad, and that was true also of the railways in Spain, the Balkans and Scandinavia. In the wake of that finance followed engineering works, public utilities like gas, water, electricity and omnibuses, mining and refining companies, banks and insurance companies and others. Meanwhile lending to the weaker governments continued, in many cases for the development of railways or other costly infrastructure.

Loans of this kind were, of course, only the first step in a developing economic relationship across the frontiers. There would often follow orders for capital goods, the appointment of managers and experts from the capital-providing country, and annual interest and amortisation payments in the opposite direction which fortified the trade links between the countries concerned. A high degree of international indebtedness would, in turn, lead to the need to co-ordinate financial policy and, if significant enough, would lead also to political subordination or dependence. A similar relationship of dependence would occur where a smaller country sold the bulk of its leading export product(s) to a single large buyer abroad. The Scandinavian countries, Spain and Portugal and the Baltic countries were all to some extent in such client status, though not necessarily to a single power: this tended to emphasise the economic interdependence in Europe and blur the distinction between the links with an outlying province within the same state and a neighbouring supplier who enjoyed nominal political independence.

What was significant was that these connections, each of which might be bilateral, formed a complete network covering the whole of Europe within which alone they made sense. This had become obvious early in such matters as posts and telegraphs; the expansion of these links, partly a function of economic growth and partly of growing integration, may best be seen in the growth of the mail handled by the Universal Postal Union: from 144 million letters conveyed in 1875, itself an enormous total, it rose to 2,500 million in 1913. Submarine cables were regulated by an international convention in 1863, all cables in 1884. After Marconi's successful patent for radio telegraphy, national rivalry threatened the usefulness of the invention which was at first employed mostly in communication at sea, but at the Berlin conference the leading powers agreed to a Radiotelegraphic Union with an obligation to use all systems. Following the *Titanic* disaster, exchanges between ships at sea were made compulsory in 1912. As early as 1879 a conference in London had adopted an international code of distress signals. In 1912 the Brussels Convention agreed on procedures to avoid collisions at sea and following the *Titanic* sinking there was a further conference in London on safety at sea. Most European countries had their own safety standards, including load line regulations, and in 1930 an international agreement was reached on load lines.

The need for such international understandings and standardisation was too self-evident to need much argument, and there were similarly obvious agreements regarding railway services. Because of their common technical origin, most

European main lines were built to the British 'standard' gauge, though Spain and Russia opted for a broader gauge. It was thus technically possible and economically desirable to run rolling stock across frontiers and co-ordination to that effect, though difficult, made sense to all. After three conferences held in Berne in 1878–86, ten states signed a convention in 1890 for conveying goods across frontiers and a central co-ordinating bureau was set up. Timetable co-ordination, begun at a conference in Munich in 1860, was completed by 1891. International express trains began to run in the 1880s. Technical matters relating to uniformity of rolling stock, loading, marking and locking goods wagons were agreed to at later conventions.

Yet the logic of international co-operation and integration of this kind had a much wider scope than merely the field of transport and communications. Medicine is a case in point. Human disease was no respecter of frontiers, as it was found to have been no respecter of class boundaries, and in the past all great plagues and epidemics had swept across the whole of Europe and indeed other continents. Developments in curative and preventive medicine, among the proudest achievements of the age, might lose their effectiveness if limited to one country, and advanced Europe was particularly concerned to prevent the spread of plagues from the East. As early as 1838 an international health council was set up in Constantinople mainly to control the hazards arising from the movement of pilgrims, and this was followed by similar action in Egypt in 1881, in Teheran and in Tangier. There followed an international sanitary convention in 1892. In 1893 the Dresden Convention agreed on internationally standardised measures, for example, on the notification of cholera in Europe. It was followed by the Paris Convention of 1894 to attack it in its overseas places of origin. In 1897 a convention in Venice agreed on measures to contain the plague. The International Office of Public Health was set up in 1907. International medical congresses were also among the most active bodies furthering European scientific collaboration.

Slavery likewise became a supranational concern, since it ultimately depended on the toleration of an international slave trade. Its abolition, driven by the highest as well as some of the most sordid sentiments affecting political decisions, might once have depended on the vigilance of the British navy alone, but later in the nineteenth century equally obviously required common action by all the major powers. The General Act against slavery passed by the Brussels conference in 1890 was signed by many nations, and an international office was set up to stamp out the evil. It is little to our purpose that the distinction between what was officially termed slavery and the kind of indentured labour and other forms of bondage widely tolerated by the Western powers was a fine one; what is significant is that an action of economic import, if it was to be effective, had to be international. The opium trade, similarly, received international attention, largely on American initiative, at the Shanghai conference of 1890. A later conference in The Hague saw several countries agree to extend the prohibition to other dangerous drugs as well.

More significant still for the future were the first attempts to deal with the conservation of natural resources on an international scale. It was clear that the preservation of fishing stocks, for example, could be enforced only when at least the major nations agreed to collaborate in it. Partial limits were agreed in The Hague in 1882 on North Sea fishing, and an agreement on the North Pacific followed in 1911. The first effective limitations on whaling were not, however, agreed until 1931, and they left many loopholes.

Agricultural agreements raised more touchy and in part political issues, and had therefore much more limited success. The sugar conventions were more in the nature of an early commodity restrictive agreement to keep up prices, of which the world was to see many more in the interwar years. An early agreement of 1864 attempted to limit the bounties paid to European sugar producers in the Western countries, but apart from leaving out the East in which output was rising sharply, it also failed to prevent France from by-passing the limitation. A more significant agreement concluded in Brussels in 1902 limited bounties and penalised non-adherents, and it set up a permanent commission, though with limited success. A conference called by the King of Italy in 1905 to control freights on food products failed, and so did the efforts of some delegates to unite Europe in a common protective tariff against the import of cheap overseas food in the interests of European farmers. However, an International Institute for Agriculture was set up in Rome which did useful scientific work. It merged into the FAO after the Second World War.

Among the most interesting of the international conventions and agencies of the day were those devoted to labour. The first conference was called in 1890 in Berlin by the German emperor, being one aspect of the peculiar German conservative interest in social questions. The representatives of fifteen nations assembled there agreed on some desirable minimum standards, on the understanding, analogous to the logic of the early Factory Acts, that those countries which enforced better conditions would undermine the competitive strength of their industries unless they could be sure that others would follow the same rules. It was very much a conference from above, about labour, rather than a meeting by labour or its representatives, and it had no practical results whatever at that stage, but it expressed implicitly the realisation of the existence of a single international labour market, at least among the advanced nations. Another conference followed in Berne in 1906, and the international association for labour legislation led directly to the establishment of the International Labour Office after the war, one of the more effective agencies attached to the League of Nations system.

It would be tedious to extend this enumeration further. What is important to stress is that these agreements and conventions, which had throughout purely practical and instrumental origins and purposes, also arose out of and contributed to a feeling of a common civilisation among the nations of Europe, together with North America. The earnest men in dark suits and with pince-nez usually well versed in one or other foreign language, who met together to represent governments, companies, or scientific societies, felt themselves to be part of an international fraternity transcending frontiers in the same way as the French-speaking army officer class in the battles of the eighteenth century shared a common feeling of belonging despite the fact that the princes whom they happened to serve at the moment were at war with each other. They were paralleled exactly by the nascent labour movement which had come together in 1889 in the Second International and cultivated a conscious feeling of class internationalism.

Despite the obvious rivalries of the powers, of which more below, they all basically belonged to the same club and they knew that it promised them benefits by keeping to the rules. Thus, to take but one example, the gold standard functioned because central banks played the game fairly and felt it paid them even to accept temporary losses in order to preserve the system. Similarly, the world was inching forward to a more effective system of international law, covering many more facets of life than before, but basing itself on the European tradition of the *ius gentium*, even though there were no overt sanctions. The keeping of gentlemen's agreements, at least among the European powers, had 'a sort of social innocence which, once lost, never returns' (Myrdal, 1956, p. 73). Progress was considered desirable by everyone, and it equalled civilised international behaviour and a recognition of growing interdependence in the economic field as much as elsewhere. It was not entirely a coincidence that the Olympic Games were revived on an international basis in 1896.

All this, however, was but one side of the coin, founded on the logic of economics and technology. Pareto, the great economist, might pronounce at the Peace Congress of 1889 in Rome that economic integration would lead later to political integration, and the Political Science Congress of 1900 might once more revive the concept of a United States of Europe, but meanwhile the political structures and particularly the great power nation state, had taken off on an entirely different path.

In part, the causes of these apparently political changes were purely technical: governments were now much more able to enforce customs regulations or tax payments, to raise and manoeuvre armies, to publish and communicate views or ordinances, or to collect statistics. Welfare provisions, Factory Acts, laws on property were all natural functions of the modern state, and professional careers, seniority, pension rights and social reform movements naturally took place within its borders. The widening extent and greater efficiency of education systems maintained by the state not only confirmed it as the obvious centre of activity and initiative, but offered unexampled means of inculcating a deep feeling of loyalty to that same state, against which other feelings of loyalty, such as to the city, the province, or the religious group, faded almost into insignificance compared with previous generations.

Thus the state became the most significant, if not sole, source of power and patronage, and by natural gravity also attracted to itself the loyalties and expectations of aid from individuals and groups who would in the past not normally have looked to their own government, or would have grouped themselves differently. Formerly, the makers or merchants might have found it more natural to combine with their fellows in their own city against those of other cities nearby, instead of

55

seeking a common interest with them against those farther away abroad; more clearly still, in ventures in less developed countries, it might be expected that those, say, who were interested in a particular mineral would combine together against the merchants, or against those interested in plantations, or against the local ruler, instead of cutting across those lines to group themselves according to their nationality. But that is what they did, and it turned economic relationships outside Europe into a field of imperialist rivalry that became one of the most significant features of the age, and one of the roots of the First World War. So difficult has it been to explain the great power imperialism of those years in terms of rational self-interest that historians to this day are fundamentally divided on explanations of its causes: these include the search for markets and raw materials, or for investment opportunities; the quest for strategic defence or offence; the spread of one or other religion; jobs for sons of the privileged classes; or the glory of soldiers and others. But in every case it is much easier to find proofs against than for these explanations. What is clear, however, is that whatever else it might be that divided or united men, in this phase of history it was the state that became the most powerful magnet to attract to itself the loyalties and expectations of aid and defence from more and more sectors of society.

Thus the changed circumstances of the 1870s led to strong demands everywhere for aid and protection by the state, in the first instance by the well-tried methods of customs tariffs. The change was most dramatic in Germany. There the turn-round in economic fortunes swung both the manufacturers, combined in 1876 in the Central Union of German Manufacturers, and the agrarians, who had hitherto been staunchly for free trade, behind a protectionist policy. Further, since direct taxes had been left to the constituent states, while the empire had to rely on indirect taxes, Bismarck looked to a revenue tariff to help him out of the need to ask the states for contributions. Besides this, changes in internal politics also made it desirable for Bismarck to break his alliance with the free traders and link up with the protectionist parties.

The result was the reimposition of a substantial tariff on both manufactures and food imports – the alliance of rye and iron. In view of the high degree of efficiency and growing penetration of world markets by German industrialists, import duties were scarcely necessary for their products though they were kept on in all subsequent changes. They yielded relatively little revenue. By contrast, agricultural output, in spite of increases in productivity, was less and less able to stand up to low-cost imports from abroad. Though tariff rates were raised in 1885 and again in 1887, imports were rising at about the same rate as in free-trade Britain, and yielded considerable tax revenue.

The trend towards growing protection was temporarily reversed by a series of treaties concluded by the new chancellor, Caprivi, beginning with the Austrian trade treaty of 1891. Many of them were timed to come to an end in 1903, by which time the agrarians, together with certain groups of protectionist industrialists, had firmly regained the upper hand. A set of new treaties concluded in 1904–5 raised tariffs on food imports particularly sharply; for imports from countries with which no treaties existed, the General Tariff Act laid down even higher duties.

In France the trend was in the same direction, but began more gently. The tariff of 1881, following on the influx of overseas grain in the late 1870s, was quite moderate, and intended largely as a bargaining counter in negotiations with other countries. A large number of treaties were made in 1881–4 on its foundation. In 1885 and 1887 agricultural protection was increased, and the new Méline tariff of 1892 ushered in a period of protectionism. Under it, agricultural *ad valorem* rates averaged 25 per cent, and industrial rates, while varying, were higher than the Caprivi rates in Germany. As in the case of Germany, particular treaties were concluded on the basis of minimum rates, and the most favoured nation clause was still widely applied. A major tariff revision in 1910 changed classifications, revised the maximum rates upwards and had a general upward tendency, though the minimum (conventional) rates were little affected.

With the exception of Britain and the Netherlands, all European countries followed a similar upward path of protectionism. In Russia the decision to levy duties in gold rather than paper roubles in 1877 represented a rise of 30–3 per cent, and there were further increases in 1881 and 1885. The Mendeleyev tariff of 1891 raised some rates still more, though some came down in what was meant to be in part a fiscal and revenue system as well as a protective one. The moderate Austro-Hungarian tariff of 1878 was made more restrictive by rises in 1882 and 1887. Italy also raised its relatively moderate tariff of 1878 in 1887 and 1894, to make it a highly protective system. The more backward countries on the periphery in the east and south of Europe tended to have higher protection still, frequently in reaction against the industrialised countries which kept out their agrarian products by high duties. In 1903–8 there was another round of tariff increases, including even some relatively liberal countries like Switzerland.

A significant feature of this period was the 'tariff wars' bringing with them particular discrimination in duties on the imports of individual countries. The most costly of them was probably the Franco-Italian tariff war which began in 1887 and, despite the reduction of Italian discrimination against France in 1889, continued until 1899. France also waged a costly tariff war with Switzerland in 1893–5 and with Spain in 1882–5. Austria engaged in a conflict with Romania which lasted, with intervals, from 1882 to 1898, and was involved in a more bitter conflict with Serbia in 1906–14. There was also a major tariff war between Germany and Canada in 1897–1900 on the issue of preference granted by the Dominion to Great Britain.

To these actions must be added subsidies, particularly to shipping and shipbuilding in such countries as France and Italy, to harm the merchants and shipbuilding firms in other countries in the interests of building up capacity at home. There were also growing restrictions on foreign migrant labour and foreign property holdings, particularly of land, though these were mild by later standards.

Whatever the immediate intentions behind these measures, one of their ultimate effects was to break up the growing interconnection of the European economy. The logic of the nation state was to assume that what would benefit one was bound to harm the other, in direct contradiction to the economic logic which was that it paid to have efficient and wealthy trading partners. The lining-up of economic interests on political lines became second nature to many. The wars of unification of Italy and Germany had made wars respectable, and although no major conflict occurred in Europe the Franco-German war of 1870, which itself was a short, sharp campaign causing relatively little loss, and colonial fighting and fighting in the periphery such as the Balkans seemed to show that European history could continue its upward movement even when some nations were at war.

No clear line emerges as there were many ups and downs, yet it does seem in retrospect that in the forty years or so before the First World War the tendencies that were breaking up the economic unity of Europe were getting stronger in relation to those that made for continuing integration, even if that drift remained hidden from contemporaries. In the end, it turned out that Norman Angell's *The Great Illusion* (1910), in which he put forward the idea that the European economies were so closely intertwined that they could not possibly go to war with each other, had fooled only himself. In 1914 a period of conflict began which was to last in different forms for thirty-one years.

5 Wars and Economic Disintegration, 1914–1945

The war of 1914–18 was in many respects the first 'total' war known to Europe. One aspect of this was that once the initial battles were over, and it had become clear that there would be no easy victory, it was the economic potential behind the fighting men that would ultimately decide the outcome. This involved the whole population instead of merely the traditional organised groups of fighting men. More significant still was the willingness of the states engaged in the conflict to use the complete panoply of powers at their command to a much greater extent than ever before, including the power to inflict blockade and other economic damage, to confiscate the property of individual citizens and intern them if they were of 'enemy' nationality, to incite minorities and colonial peoples on the other side to revolt and, of course, to prohibit all intercourse with subjects of the enemy states. The maintenance of personal and even of some economic relationships which had been normal in earlier wars had become quite unthinkable after 1914.

Thus the links between the different parts of Europe, built up with so much labour over the years, were ruthlessly broken. The belligerents seemed almost to enjoy inflicting hardships and costs on their own citizens, if only they could be sure that citizens of the enemy states would suffer even more. Enormous propaganda machines, building on the foundation of mutual hatred laid by patriots and nationalist societies even before the war, were engaged to depict the other side as inhuman, subhuman and unfit to be considered fellow Europeans. Governments did not hesitate to break any of the rules that got in the way. The neutrality of Belgium was violated, most prewar conventions were broken, or kept only as long as it suited current purposes, and the needs of war were proclaimed superior to all other obligations. As the juggernauts of hatred began to roll, the gossamer threads of international understanding spun before the war parted with hardly a tremor. Even the Socialist International, so brave in its condemnation of war and expression of working-class internationalism before 1914, dissolved at once into warlike national sections with but few exceptions. Scientific societies, voluntary organisations and churches were no match either for the power of the modern state at war to bury all other human links under its own weight and momentum.

Some links were strengthened within the two groups of belligerents, the Allies and the Central Powers. Thus the Allies developed a common shipping control and joint supply services, there was some specialisation of production between them, and there was, of course, strategic collaboration. But it could not be said that any state gave up much of its sovereignty to its alliance. Loyalty to one's own government became infinitely stronger than loyalty to allies, and one country, Italy, after much hesitation, even left one set of allies and joined the other, without causing too much confusion among its citizens.

Quite apart from this sharpening of the focus of national patriotism while all other human relationships shaded into a weak undifferentiated background, the sheer needs of total war required a vast extension of the power of the modern state over the economy. Currency and financial controls were imposed at once almost everywhere, and existing controls over trade were also tightened up. Conscription ended all freedom of labour mobility, at least for able-bodied men of military age, and the migration of others was also made difficult. Though there were inter-Allied loans, they were made by governments, at least in Europe, and the freedom of movement of capital was restricted even within each country. The world became inward-looking; those who had preached autarky for the sake of strategic advantage seemed to have been borne out by events; and governments sprouted measures and practices of control undreamt-of in previous ages, to be used again after the war when occasion demanded.

The peace settlement as it was worked out from 1919 onwards appeared to be a triumph of national self-determination. The Austro-Hungarian Empire as well as much of the Russian and Turkish empires were broken up and reshaped into nation states, and even though these and other frontier adjustments tended to favour the victors and diminish the territory of the losers, including that of the new Soviet Union, there was always at least the nominal justification of the principle of nationality – except perhaps in the Polish corridor which was purely strategic.

Yet it would be hard to sustain the view that the principle of the independent nation state, proclaimed implicitly with so much fervour in Wilson's fourteen points on which the postwar settlement was in theory shaped, was a progressive principle in the conditions of 1919. Persecution of national minorities and discriminatory action against them began almost at once. Large numbers of refugees were forced to move across frontiers, a feature all too characteristic of Europe in the age of disintegration, contrasting in their fear and despair with the hope and anticipation which characterised the migrant in happier days of open frontiers. Between Turks and Greeks the treatment of minorities turned into massacres, and in the end the newly formed League of Nations helped to transplant 1·3 million Greeks from Asia Minor in return for 400,000 Turks, to end the killing and the persecution. Others who had nowhere to go to, like the Armenians, continued to be massacred in the postwar wave of xenophobia.

As a large number of new states arose in Europe as the outcome of the war, one estimate put the length of the new customs frontiers at 11,000 kilometres, or 7,000 miles. Given the manner of their creation, it was perhaps inevitable that in their early stages these countries should be governed by fervent nationalists, mostly men of little practical experience, to whom national glory was far more important than the economic welfare of their populations. In the upshot, their actions in the economic field proved nothing less than disastrous, and contributed materially to the poverty and the depression of the interwar years, and the eventual descent of much of Europe into barbarism.

The beginnings were not propitious. Most of the new countries which stretched in an irregular belt from Esthonia in the north to Yugoslavia, Albania and an enlarged Greece in the south were poor and backward. With the exception of Czechoslovakia and the rump of German-speaking Austria, both of which were industrialised though they also had much agriculture of variable efficiency, they were largely agrarian countries at a low level of productivity. Such industry, public utilities, commercial and financial organisations as they had were geared to different, prewar trading and currency systems and, being brutally severed by the new frontiers, would have needed the most careful nursing to readjust. Thus ironworks and railways were found on one side of a new frontier, coalmines and repair shops on the other; spinning on this side, weaving on that. Over some stretches the railways wound in and out of the dividing line, in others their natural junctions were on the wrong side of the border. Towns found their agricultural supplies cut off by customs barriers, factories had their traditional bank and even their shareholders abroad. But instead of getting together to make the most of the limited resources available the new governments did their best to destroy what was left.

Almost at once there were claims and counter-claims for property, there was expropriation and retaliation. In direct contrast to the logic of the nineteenth century, where railways led countries to collaborate for mutual benefit, now no country in the region dared to send its trains across the border, for fear that they might be seized: goods in such trade as survived were laboriously transhipped at the frontier. It was as if the new governments wanted to neutralise the advantages of civilisation.

These were initial pinpricks only, some of them of a temporary nature. More serious was the immediate erection of high tariff walls between areas that were natural economic partners, as well as the determination, against all economic logic, of each of these states to industrialise and become self-sufficient as quickly as possible. In view of their poverty, technical backwardness and the small size of their home markets, this meant that valuable resources were wasted in building up utterly inefficient plants which henceforth had to be protected and subsidised, depriving the population of the benefits of cheap manufactured imports as well as preventing the overdue modernisation of their agriculture. In this way the countries broke not only the trading relations between themselves, but also those with Western Europe which before the war had formed their market for agrarian products and had supplied them with agricultural machinery and technology, with railway equipment and with development capital. Attempts were made at Ponteroso in 1921, and intermittently in 1922–5, to get the Austro-Hungarian successor states to end their mutual discrimination and lower tariffs to each other, but they foundered on national exclusiveness.

Meanwhile the rest of Europe itself was in no hurry to return to trade normalcy. Germany, as the loser, was obliged to give the Allies unilateral most-favoured-nation treatment and was strictly limited as to the protection it could maintain, but its tariffs went up substantially in 1923. The others, notably Britain, kept on many of the protective measures introduced during the war. By the mid-1920s, when conditions had returned to a fair degree of normalcy, most sets of tariffs and commercial treaties were revised, and while it is extremely difficult to compare one set of rates with another unless all the rates move in the same direction, the general tendency was for the rates to settle at a level well above that of 1913. Some countries developed high tariffs as bargaining weapons – *tarifs de combat* – which might not come down when there was no reciprocity. Moreover trade treaties showed a significant tendency to be of shorter duration than prewar: of 180 treaties concluded between 1920 and August 1926 all but twenty-seven could be altered at the end of one year.

Meanwhile there was another effect of the war which was coming into prominence: this was the disruption of the European monetary system. War finance had led to the depreciation of all currencies, with a tendency for the depreciation to worsen as one moved east. After the war, far from improving, conditions deteriorated and in several countries went completely out of control. In Britain and the neutrals, prices at no point rose to more than two and a half times the prewar levels, and even in Belgium, France, Italy and Finland they rose no more than six- to eight-fold. In less fortunate areas, such as Bulgaria, Greece, Romania, Yugoslavia, Portugal and Esthonia, they rose between fifteen and eighty times. Apart from Soviet Russia, the countries in which the value of money disappeared completely were Austria,

Hungary, Poland and Germany. In each of them, the increases in prices were to be counted in millions per cent.

The rehabilitation of these currencies took until 1925–7, by which time something like stable relationships had been restored. But in the process countries had learnt to manipulate the exchange value of their currency for protective purposes, thus adding a weapon to the armoury of protection and a method of disrupting the European economy which was to be used on a large scale in the 1930s. Deflation as enforced by some caused bankruptcies, unemployment and distortion as between sheltered trades that did not operate under threat of foreign competition, like building, and the unsheltered trades that did.

Under the influence of these and other factors the development of trade began to lag behind the development of other economic activity. Even by 1925, when the population of Eastern Europe (excluding Russia) stood at 103 (1913 = 100) and output of raw materials and foodstuffs stood at 102, the quantum of trade was only 82; for Western Europe at that time the figures were 105, 108 and 99 respectively. For the world as a whole manufacturing in 1926/9 stood at 139 (1913 = 100), and quantum of world trade for primary products at 113 and for manufactured articles at 104; the respective figures for 1936/8 were 185, 119 and 92. In other words, between 1926/9 and 1936/8, manufacturing output rose by 33 per cent, trade in primary products by 3·5 per cent, and trade in manufactured articles actually fell by 13 per cent. The law of the diminishing proportion of trade seemed truly to have taken over.

There was one further effect of the war which had a significant influence on international economic relations. That was the changes in the mutual indebtedness among the victors and the reparations imposed on Germany. Before the war it had been the advanced manufacturing nations who had been the international creditors; France and Germany as well as Belgium and Holland being among the exporters of capital together with Great Britain. During the war, France, Italy and other European nations fell heavily into debt to Britain and the USA, while their own loans to Russia had to be written off. Germany was burdened by huge reparations even after these were regulated by the Dawes Plan from 1924, and its large annual payments (which in turn allowed countries like France to service its own debts to its allies) could be kept going only by raising simultaneously new loans in the USA.

The large-scale indebtedness of advanced nations found to exist in the 1920s was a new phenomenon, but the indebtedness of food and raw material producers, except for the USA which had now become the world's leading international lender, continued as before. These debt relationships and obligations to meet annual payments added an element of instability to the financial system. When prices began to fall primary product prices fell more than other prices in the 1920s, and in the 1930s they collapsed catastrophically. In those conditions the obligation to make annual payments fixed in money terms became the more burdensome in real terms as the power to make them shrunk. They led to national defaults and bankruptcies as well as to savage deflation and restrictions of imports as methods of dealing with the balance-of-payments problem. This added a further impetus to the downward spiral of trade.

Thus the producers of food and raw materials, in Europe and overseas, were faced with the problem of poverty and deficits in their balance of payments as their relative export prices fell and their terms of trade deteriorated, but this was of little benefit to the industrialised countries after the crash of 1929 when depression spread around the world. They were faced with unemployment aggravated by the fact that they could not sell their products to their traditional and now impoverished customers. It was not difficult to show in those conditions that whatever other consequences might arise from protection, it would at least protect work and help to 'export unemployment'. Thus both industrial and primary producers, though for different reasons, saw immediate relief in preventing imports or raising exports. No country could control its exports, since they were affected by the protective actions of others, but imports were under the control of each government. The remedy for unbalance was thus everywhere to cut, rather than expand. Each cut led to further retaliation, and the upshot was the break-up of the world economy and the European economy into hostile and embattled fortresses representing the individual states.

There were therefore now two powerful forces at work for the disruption of the delicate network of European trade. One was the traditional pressure from uncompetitive industries and from high-cost agriculture asking to be preserved from the competion of low-cost imports, and this was a plea which could now be strengthened by reference to heavy unemployment and the immediate hope of creating employment behind tariff walls. The other, and essentially newer argument – though it had been familiar in theory since the beginning of the nineteenth century – was based on the total balance of payments, and the inability of some countries to meet their total obligations abroad, with a consequent threat to the whole of their currency and financial system.

The currency disorders of the 1930s thus took on a new significance in this context. In the 1920s something like an international gold standard had been re-established though not without difficulty. Sweden had returned to gold in 1924, Britain in 1925, France in 1926, Belgium in 1927 and Italy in 1928. Weaker economies that could not afford the full gold standard were encouraged to settle for a 'gold exchange' standard, tying their currency not to a gold reserve but to a reserve of another currency based on gold, which was much less costly for them, though it greatly added to the instability of the countries fully on gold. While that system lasted it helped, as it had in the nineteenth century, to provide a stable and secure framework within which international economic relations could thrive. By the same token, the collapse of the system did massive damage to these relations.

Among the major currencies the pound sterling with its low reserves and overextended obligations both to Britain's own extensive trade network and to the maintenance of a number of weak centres in Europe was the first to crack. In 1931 Britain went off gold and the exchange value of sterling fell at once by 20–30 per cent. Although a number of dependent economies devalued with sterling, the group as a whole gained immediate competitive advantages over the rest of the world, and this was fortified by the imposition of protection in Britain, reversing a policy under which Britain had prospered for eighty years. In 1932, also, the Ottawa Agreement provided for preferential treatment among members of the Commonwealth and Empire, and this led in the sequel to a diversion from trade with outsiders to trade within that area, though perhaps to a lesser extent than had been hoped. Thus the devaluation of sterling and the bundle of related measures put up high barriers between one major block and the rest of the world trading network.

Germany had been under pressure earlier than Britain and had survived for a time by savage deflationary measures that helped to raise the level of unemployment and the destruction of capital to an extent that it overstrained the democratic fabric of society. Voters flocked to the extreme parties by the million, and in January 1933 Hitler and his Nazi Party took over control. Their social policies, but above all their policies of rearmament and of preparing the German economy for war, helped to diminish unemployment, but they put the payments balance under intolerable strain. Germany solved that problem by thorough and ever-increasing controls over trade and over foreign payments. A complex system developed, under which payments to importers were frozen and released only at a discount or in return for exports from Germany. But since such methods could be applied with much greater force to countries that had a trading surplus with Germany than to those on whose markets the Germans themselves depended, differential rates had to be applied until in the end the 'Mark' lost its meaning in international terms, there being a whole series of different Marks available at different exchange values; the system also lent itself easily to bilateral trade and clearing agreements. Germany had to all intents and purposes been removed from the free international trading network.

The USA, always a protectionist country, had increased its tariff rates to prohibitive heights by the Hawley–Smoot tariff of 1930, though this made little difference to its unemployment rate and its bankruptcies, which were among the worst in the world. In 1933 the USA also went off gold, though the country held a large part of the world's gold reserves which it had accumulated since the war, and the dollar was devalued to roughly the same extent as the pound sterling. With the US dollar, again, a number of dependent currencies devalued also.

This left France and its 'gold bloc' high and dry, their prices overvalued in international terms. To protect their interests, a system of quotas was superimposed on the tariff and before long took the place of the traditional system of customs duties to prevent the import of foreign produce and manufactures. Quotas, whether on imports or on the composition of consumption, such as the limits on foreign grain that might be mixed in by French millers or the proportion of foreign films that might be shown by British exhibitors, are a much more rigid form of exclusion than tariffs, which only affect prices and therefore allow a good deal of flexibility. They also lend themselves much more to bilateral agreements for that trade which is permitted at all. At least twelve countries in Europe were using quotas as trade restrictions by 1932.

The franc bloc finally also went off gold in 1936, and although the controllers of the three major currencies, the US dollar, the pound sterling and the French franc, then came to a 'Tripartite Agreement' not to devalue their currencies further without prior consultation, and in fact a certain stability in parities was secured, the world had clearly broken up into major economic regions in which currency manipulation helped to divert and limit international commerce. Bearing in mind that the Soviet Union had also a completely controlled, artificial and by prewar standards insignificant exchange and trading system, there was now little left of the free European trading network based on a single gold standard that had evolved over previous generations.

The smaller countries in the West, notably Switzerland, the Netherlands and the Scandinavian countries, were by their very size precluded from seeking complete autarky, nor were they normally strong enough to enforce favourable terms in bilateral treaties. They therefore held to rather more liberal policies and helped to turn the world slightly in the same liberal direction after 1936.

The smaller countries in the East, however, had no such option open to them. Heavily in debt, dependent on exports the prices of which were falling fast and which were in any case being excluded from their traditional markets by the pressure of farmers in the West, they could only react by the most massive exchange controls, by trade restrictions and by defaults, each of which restricted their trade further. In a system in which

each country could generally restrict unchallenged imports from countries with which it had an import balance and could frequently oblige those countries to take more of its products, it exposed itself to retaliations if it attempted to restrict imports from other countries. The restrictions imposed were therefore largely discriminatory and for this and other reasons tended to balance transactions with each country separately rather than in the aggregate. Multilateral trade was thus reduced and replaced by bilateral trade. (League of Nations, 1942, p. 9)

Bilateral trade, with clearing (i.e. balancing) agreements, thus became the norm in Eastern Europe, and in default of any help by other major economies it was mainly Germany with which countries in that region came to exchange their goods. In this way they became increasingly dependent, politically as well as economically, on the Nazi state.

Bilateral trade was becoming the rule in the rest of Europe also, however. One tabulation listing the proportion of the trade balance of certain countries with countries with which bilateral treaties had been made showed the following change in percentage terms between 1931 and 1934 (Friedman, 1974, p. 49):

	1931	*1934*
France	69·1	95·6
Switzerland	42·7	55·9
Italy	33·4	81·2
Hungary	36·9	83·6
Bulgaria	3·7	46·2
Romania	59·3	89·8

While the depression thus helped to break up the European economy, it tended to fortify the inner cohesion of countries themselves. Unemployment and other welfare and benefit schemes on the one hand, and currency manipulation, protection and subsidy schemes on the other, served to

73

emphasise the large economic role now played by the state in the economic life of the people. Prosperity, even survival, for each firm and each industry in turn, came to depend ever less on success in the market place, and ever more on the political skill of attracting government support of one kind or another. All this clearly tended to increase the consciousness of interdepence within the national community and enlarged the distance to communities on the other side of the border. It also brought to the fore, once more, the efforts to save imports by heavy expenditure on import substitution, particularly the drive in agrarian societies, inside Europe and overseas, to build up their own industrial base.

Under these new conditions it was no longer possible, as it had largely been before 1914, to see any economic logic in the steady progress of European economic integration while it was in the nature of the sovereign state to split Europe apart on national lines. For the functions of the state had necessarily spread to take on so many aspects of economic life that the isolation of economic market foreces from political authority even in a purely theoretical sphere no longer made much sense. At the same time economic developments themselves, like the behaviour of food and raw material prices, or the collapse of overall demand and the rise of mass unemployment, led many to question the earlier assumption that the world was becoming more prosperous albeit with certain ups and downs, and was growing more closely together.

Moreover, there was a certain schizophrenia in the policies of governments, particularly in the West. For while they acted in the manner described with supreme national egotism, as if the interests of foreign citizens were of no account whatever, and did their best to isolate the different national economies from each other, they were at the same time well aware of the costs of such measures and of the potential benefits of international collaboration and of economic integration.

Measures to secure the latter were repeatedly devised by the leading statesmen of the day in one conference after another. It was only when these proposals were taken home and examined in the framework of national policies that national politicians (frequently the same men) failed to back or ratify them.

The financial conference held in Brussels in 1920 was the first to be called by the newly formed League of Nations. It urged the end of restrictions and discrimination, but had little effect beyond leading to some regularisation of bills of lading. The failure of the Ponteroso conference of 1921 to promote economic collaboration among the Austro-Hungarian successor states has already been noted. In 1922 the Genoa conference again pronounced in favour of removing obstacles to trade and of providing credit for the weaker nations in order to restore something of the prewar economic position, while the Barcelona conference of 1921 and the Genoa and Geneva conferences of 1923 were concerned with the freedom of transport.

Although there was some return to normalcy in the mid-1920s, particularly in the financial field, and many special restrictions were repealed, it cannot be said that these efforts on an international scale bore much fruit, unless we assume that without them things might have been even worse. Another conference, held in Geneva in 1927, at which twenty-nine countries including the leading European nations, the USA and Japan, participated, came to an agreement 'to abolish within a period of six months all import and export prohibitions or restrictions and not thereafter to impose any such prohibitions or restrictions'. However, from the start numerous exceptions were permitted, and others were added in a supplementary agreement arrived at in 1928. By 1929, when the agreement was to have come into force, there were not enough ratifications to get it off the ground. A few countries adopted some of the rules in 1930, but by 1934 all had denounced them.

Also in 1927 one of the two major world economic conferences of the interwar period met and, rather to the surprise of most delegates, achieved unanimous expressions of agreement for freer trade relationships. Figures were produced to show to what extent trade had failed to recover its prewar position and had dropped behind output. The 'excessive nationalism' and the attempts at national autarky following the postwar settlements were deplored. Once more the hope was expressed that prohibitions and restrictions would be ended, discrimination of foreigners and legal privileges of nationals abolished, and trade and transport eased. Once more no tangible results followed.

The world economic crisis which broke in 1929 was therefore not responsible for the failure to return to the more open economic policies of the prewar years, though it certainly aggravated the tendency to national exclusiveness and the attempt by each country to solve its problems at the expense of all the others. International efforts in the direction of greater liberalism continued, however. Thus there were two conferences, in 1930 and 1931, in the hope of arriving at a tariff truce, or, in other words, at agreements not to increase protection; and in 1932 there was the Stresa conference which tried to liberalise economic relations among the Danubian countries; but all remained fruitless.

In 1930 the Bank for International Settlements had been set up in Basle by some central banks and three American banks. It was intended largely to deal with German reparations which almost at once thereafter ceased to be paid, but also to maintain some contacts in place of the now defunct gold standard and to organise the transfer of gold between countries. It was of little real account and its collaboration with the Germans excluded it from the Bretton Woods postwar schemes, but it ultimately re-emerged within the European payments system.

The second major international monetary and economic

conference of the interwar years was held in London in 1933. By that time the world had experienced more than three years of crisis and mass unemployment, currency collapses and defaults on reparations and other international debts, and the Hitler takeover in Germany. There was therefore a more desperate mood to break through the traditional barriers and attempt novel solutions; at the same time there were also mountainous new barriers to be overcome. The main issue appeared to be monetary, since the recent devaluation of the dollar had added competitive lowering of the exchange value of currencies to the weapons disrupting trade, and the story has often been told how President Roosevelt's refusal to enter into any agreement on currency stabilisation effectively torpedoed the conference. In the event, it broke up without even coming to the kind of pious if ineffective conclusion that had emerged from earlier similar meetings.

After the American Reciprocal Tariff Agreements Act of 1934 which allowed the USA to offer some mutual concessions, mainly to American and the smaller European countries, and the Tripartite Agreement of 1936 between the leading Western economic blocs there was a distinct easing of defensive and protective attitudes. The Van Zeeland Report of 1938 was part of that movement. However, the economic decline after the moderate business peak of 1937 led to renewed restrictions in practice while international meetings still sought to find ways of moving in the opposite direction.

There is perhaps one pointer to the fact that this sorry divergence between what governments apparently considered desirable and what they were in fact doing was not so much a result of political jockeying (though it did become so in the later 1930s) as of economic logic once internal prosperity within the state became the sole overriding aim. It is to be found in the fate which befell the various efforts to form regional combinations. The abortive attempts to persuade the Danubian countries into some form of economic co-operation have already been mentioned and there were similar failures to arrive at economic agreements in the Little Entente in 1933 and the Baltic and Balkan Ententes in 1934. The French veto of the proposed German-Austrian Customs Union in 1931, itself a reaction to a rather desperate crisis in both countries, was not the only intrusion of power politics into this story. The attempt at Oslo in 1930 to form a Northern Customs Union and in Ouchy in 1932 to launch a similar scheme for Holland, Belgium and Luxembourg were in effect vetoed by Britain on the grounds that they would violate the most-favoured-nation clause. Thus political and economic muscle was used to exact small temporary advantages at great cost to others. Only the insignificant links of Belgium–Luxembourg (1922), Switzerland–Liechtenstein (1924) and Italy–San Marino–Albania (1939) went through.

Meanwhile grand schemes for European unification and integration were by no means absent, but they became increasingly utopian, since not only did they have no relation to the political realities of Europe, but those realities were clearly moving away from such solutions rather than towards them. Count Coudenhove-Kalergi, a man of suitably transnational origins, gained perhaps the widest echo for his Paneuropa movement, supported by a journal of the same name issued from Vienna and following his successful book first published in 1923. There were also numerous other initiatives right up to Clarence K. Streit's *Union Now* which appeared at the eleventh hour in 1939 and proposed a federation of fifteen democracies including the USA.

The initiative which came closest to the seats of power was that of the Frenchman, Aristide Briand, sometime prime minister and a constant champion of European economic union. In 1929 he launched a major proposal for a form of federal union for Europe which was submitted officially by the

French to the League of Nations in 1930. It was not without its ambiguity, since it not only held that the 'peoples of Europe ... must establish a permanent regime of joint responsibility for the rational organisation of Europe', but at the same time maintained that it 'must be realised on the plane of their absolute sovereignty and complete political independence'. However, it was taken seriously enough by the twenty-six governments which replied, and by such stout defenders of the European idea as Edouard Herriot in France and Gustav Stresemann in Germany. That initiative, also, had no tangible results, in part because its leading protagonists died or fell from power, and in part because the depression imposed other, more immediately effective solutions; possibly there was also the suspicion that Briand's plan might be merely a hidden scheme for buttressing French hegemony over Europe.

It is noteworthy that support for these and other schemes, though it might come from many countries, came from only narrow circles in each: from authors, politicians, academics, or diplomats. They lacked any form of mass support, nor could these essentially voluntary movements even begin to match the massive propaganda for nationalism and xenophobic hatred which schools, press and political parties constantly poured out as their normal stock in trade.

Superimposed on the breakdown of the former intra-European economic links and relationships, for which the war with its changed boundaries and the world economic depression must be at least in part held responsible, there was another factor which had also arisen at least indirectly from the war. Whereas before 1914 there were certain things that civilised and would-be civilised countries simply did not do, that is to say, there were limits accepted in the interest of preserving a system which on the whole had done well by all, there were now dissatisfied powers, above all Germany, Italy and Japan, which considered that their gains from preserving a civilised world system were so small, and the gap between their potential and their actual political status so wide, that it would pay them to defy the rules. Long-standing patterns of international behaviour were now ignored with increasing frequency, treaties disregarded, promises broken without even a pretence of justification, brutal pressures and ultimately wars were unleashed, and all in a way that showed that some countries no longer wished or needed to be considered 'respectable'. In turn, this reflected the brutal lawlessness, out of line with the growth over the centuries of public civilised behaviour, within their own boundaries by the new political leaders of these irredentist or, as Moritz Bonn called them, 'unsaturated' powers (Bonn, 1938, p. 396). Even in their dress, the jack-booted quasi-uniform of the street fighter, they showed that they placed no value on creating a good impression or on being held to be respectable. A philosophy which begins by coveting the lands and wealth of other people in Europe because they are inferior human beings is clearly not conducive to the kind of gradual growing together which the European economies had experienced before 1914.

Thus it was that when much of the continent fell into the hands of Germany and her Axis partners in the course of the war of 1939–45, there was no question of taking the opportunity of a genuine unification of Europe. The Nazi 'New Order' and still more the 'European Congress of November 1941' were a sham. The non-German territories were simply treated as booty and devastated, robbed, or just exploited as reservoirs of cheap labour, all in the interest of the German war machine and the German consumer. Which of these methods was adopted depended on a mixture of genuine economic calculations as to maximising the benefits for German production and on the irrational classification of nations according to the fascists' arbitrary racist schemes.

6 Integration in a Divided Europe

The war of 1939–45 was fought out in part by rousing the fiercest nationalist passions; at the same time it was also an ideological war in which both sets of protagonists came to repudiate the political motivations and the economic policies of the interwar period. As the Axis powers occupied one country after another, resistance to them by governments in exile, within the underground in Europe, and even in the prisoner of war and the concentration camps became an international and transnational movement.

The men of the resistance were entitled and perhaps were even obliged to have their utopia and the utopia would be one of a European continent in which the nations had ceased to war with each other and had learned to live in peace and human dignity. The Ventotene Manifesto of July 1941, the work of Italian resisters under Altiero Spinelli, was perhaps the best-known expression of these views, denouncing nationalist egotism and proposing a federal solution for Europe after the war. It led directly to the Geneva Declaration of July 1944, the most authoritative statement to come out of continental Europe at the time, which accepted the principles of the Atlantic Charter, but at the same time envisaged a single federal structure for Europe, as well as social reforms, the establishment of democratic rule everywhere, and the access of all countries to the sea. Significantly, it was not only the movements from Western Europe and from Germany herself that were represented there, but also resistance leaders from countries in Eastern Europe, and the federal structure proposed was naturally to include the eastern half of the continent.

The 'Big Four' who actually settled the peace terms were less impressed by these European sentiments; apart from the temporary occupation and permanent weakening of Germany, and the westward expansion of the Soviet Union, they seemed to be intent on returning as closely as possible to the status quo of pre-1936, thus legitimising the 1919 settlement as well as their own official war aims. Nevertheless, the sentiments of the resistance, which in some form or other expressed the aspirations of large numbers of fellow citizens who were neither very active nor very conscious politically, were not entirely without effect on the subsequent history of Europe.

After 1946 European movements and congresses shot out of the ground at a rate far greater than at any previous time in history. The Hague Congress of 1948 was only the most influential of these. Article 1 of its declaration advised 'the nations of Europe to create an economic and political union', and Article 3 obliged them 'to transfer and merge some portion of their sovereign rights so as to secure common political and economic action for the integration and proper development of their common resources'. As early as May 1946 Paul van Zeeland and Joseph Retinger had attempted to establish an Independent (later European) League for Economic Co-operation, envisaging a customs union of the Western nations, and in 1948 Retinger was among those who helped to call the Hague Congress. Out of it grew the European movement under Churchill, Léon Blum, De Gasperi and Henri Spaak, as well as the Council of Europe, a formal organisation of ten governments, though the British succeeded in much reducing its significance.

The unifying sentiments emerging out of Europe influenced events also by a second route, via the great powers themselves. Churchill's speech in Zurich in 1946, calling for a United States of Europe, made a great impression in the English-speaking world, though not for the time being on the governments, but the readiness with which the Marshall Plan administration took to the notion of European economic co-operation had been nourished by these developments in Europe which also helped to make it viable. A third line of influence stretches directly to the statesmen like de Gasperi, Schuman, Jean Monnet, Spaak and Adenauer who arose out of this milieu and then went on to lay the foundation of the economic integration of Western Europe as it actually took place.

Events moved towards economic integration along two planes. One was on a worldwide scale, culminating in the formation of the United Nations and its various affiliated and related organisations, such as the Food and Agricultural Organisation (1945), the World Health Organisation (1948) and the Economic Commission for Europe (1947), which covered both Eastern and Western Europe. Among the most significant agencies on a world scale was the International Monetary Fund (IMF) set up at the Bretton Woods conference of 1944, which was designed to overcome one of the most pernicious causes of economic disintegration before the war, currency instability and unbalance. It created, in effect, a buffer of loanable funds which was available to member countries who found themselves in temporary balance-of-payments difficulties. This line of credit available to countries in trouble formed a valuable concession and it could be used to enforce the IMF's 'rules', which included a ban on unilateral competitive devaluations such as countries had learned to use as forms of protection before the war. Although by its nature it was unable to help a country in persistent unbalance with the rest of the world, it turned out to be highly successful in preventing temporary embarrassments from having long-term consequences, and at the same time, and perhaps more importantly, it provided a framework within which countries even if they had to break the rules, did so only after consultation and usually with the consent of the rest. It ensured, in other words, that the kind of competitive anarchy which had helped to break up the prewar world system of commerce was no longer respectable, as it was no longer necessary. At the same time the International Bank for Reconstruction and Development (World Bank) was set up, with a similar membership. In view of rapid reconstruction in Europe, that part of its function was in little demand and it became essentially an institution for lending development sums to poorer countries, mostly outside Europe.

Linked with these two bodies, the Havana Charter envisaged an International Trade Organisation which would buttress the prohibition on unilateral devaluation by making the unilateral imposition of tariffs or discrimination in trade illegal, on pain of being excluded from the organisation. This plan was part of the same drive towards a postwar settlement that would make a repetition of the economic and therefore political disasters of the 1930s impossible, and it is therefore not without significance that it was never ratified by the main powers, so that it did not come into operation. In 1947 the General Agreement on Tariffs and Trade (GATT) was concluded, with a less stringent set of rules under which countries undertook not to increase tariffs and restrictions against each other and to maintain the most-favoured-nation clause, except within empires. Commodity agreements were permitted in certain cases, and so were measures of self-defence in the event of balance-of-payments difficulties. The agreement has been at least in part effective in limiting rises in tariffs and encouraging reductions, including those on a worldwide scale under the 'Kennedy round'.

On the European plane effective moves towards economic and political integration were first initiated by the Marshall Plan of 1947. This plan proposed to give economic aid to Europe on a large scale in order to help the European economies which were potentially sound but needed temporary aid to make good some of the war destruction and prime the pumps of industry. Its method was to finance vital imports from the USA that could not otherwise be paid for. It was a scheme the success of which must have astonished even its authors and it set Western Europe firmly on a path of rapid recovery. Beyond this, it had the further significance that its motivation was anti-Russian and anti-communist and it set out to achieve its aims directly by grouping the countries of Western Europe firmly in an anti-Soviet alliance, and indirectly because it was sustained by the belief that poverty would favour communism and prosperity would diminish its impact. Since Eastern Europe was by that time firmly in the hands of communist governments friendly to the Soviet Union, what emerged was that the 'unification' of what is often inaccurately referred to as 'Europe' was achieved only by splitting Europe in two, deliberately and irreversibly, at least for years to come.

In return for economic aid in the form of dollars and dollar goods, the US administration demanded from the recipient countries moves towards closer economic collaboration, with something like the American model in mind. As a result, the Organisation for European Economic Co-Operation (OEEC) was set up in 1948 by sixteen countries and turned out to be remarkably resilient. Possibly its most potent achievement was the creation of a series of payments schemes, of which the last, in 1950, was the European Payments Union (EPU) ensuring that the dollar shortage would not prevent the maximum development of trade among the European countries, since their mutual indebtedness could be settled by intra-European means without endangering the holdings of each of hard currencies like the dollar.

Beyond this, however, the economic effects of this grandiose and politically motivated scheme proved to be minimal. It kept Western Europe firmly in the anti-Soviet camp and helped to strengthen the military alliance under the North Atlantic Treaty Organisation (NATO), and it certainly contributed to keeping the subsequent moves towards genuine economic integration wholly in Western Europe. But genuine progress had to wait for initiatives on practical, purely economic issues.

The first moves in that direction were made for the purpose of bringing together the main coal and steel industries. In their case the hurdles set up by political boundaries had in the past proved to be particularly costly and illogical and in addition it had been precisely these industries which had become a focus of international hostility and national armaments and war-mongering. It was therefore appropriate that those concerned with economic needs, as well as those eager to maintain the European feelings of a common destiny made so clearly manifest in the resistance movement, should welcome moves to overcome the legacies of the past in this sector.

The working idea originated in a memorandum of 1950 by Jean Monnet, the genius behind French postwar planning. A year later, in May 1951, the European Coal and Steel Community was set up by the Treaty of Paris and it began to operate in 1952. There were six member states, France, Western Germany, Italy, Belgium, the Netherlands and Luxembourg, Britain having refused to join. The object was to abolish all protection and discrimination in the trade in coal, iron and steel and various products of these between the Six, and under an administrative structure which gave a great deal of autonomy to the committed 'Europeans' running the scheme it proved to be remarkably successful.

The initiative was not allowed to die. In 1955 the Messina conference of foreign ministers decided to investigate the possibilities of extending the common market idea to all commodities. The Spaak Report, completed in 1956, provided a blueprint, and in 1957 the Treaty of Rome established the grandiosely named European Economic Community (EEC), still consisting of the same six countries only, but now embracing almost the whole of their economic activity. Over a period of twelve years (slightly shortened in practice) they were to form a complete customs union, making trade wholly free within and maintaining a common tariff to the outside world. To buttress the realities of creating a true large single economic unit a whole series of supplementary measures was taken or planned. These included a social fund, an investment bank, the encouragement of labour mobility by gradual alignment of social services and a common subsidy scheme for agricultural produce.

This is not the place to trace in detail what has proved to be the largest customs union ever created and the most powerful agency for the integration of Europe so far. Until arrested by the oil crisis of 1973, the members of the Community enjoyed unprecedented economic prosperity and a remarkably high economic growth rate, though opinion differs widely as to whether that success was caused or at least aided by the formation of the Common Market, or whether it merely continued the previous tendency which was undoubtedly there before the Market was formed. Between 1958 and 1970 trade within the EEC increased by 630 per cent, showing the remarkable progress of integration, and completely reversing, as indeed had the whole of world trade, the interwar trend of the declining share of trade. Such economic successes undoubtedly kept the momentum going towards further steps to integration in other fields, economic, social and political. But it is of equal significance that they also tended to take the pressure off governments which had come together, in the first instance, partly out of a position of weakness. Meetings within the Community, particularly at ministerial level, came to take on the aura of national egotism, of beggar-my-neighbour policies, of diplomatic horse-trading, so familiar in prewar European conferences. This was so above all as regards the major bone of contention, the one item of policy which was not at all a necessary part of the initial concept but has now become by far the costliest item in its budget, the Common Agricultural Policy (CAP).

The Nordic countries began consultations on social policy as early as 1945. In 1946 they set up their joint airline, SAS, and there followed agreements on easing labour mobility in 1954, on social security in 1955 and a Treaty of Co-operation in 1962. The Organisation of Nordic Economic Co-operation (NORDEK) was established in 1969.

More ambitious was the attempt by a group of countries including Great Britain, the three Scandinavian countries of Denmark, Sweden and Norway, Austria, Switzerland and Portugal to match the Economic Community without going beyond internal free trade among themselves. They therefore excluded any further aims of political or social integration, and even stopped short of a common outer tariff. On this basis the European Free Trade Association (EFTA) was formed by the Treaty of Stockholm in 1959 and operated from 1960. Neither its degree of economic linkage nor its growth rate was as satisfactory as those of the Common Market, and Britain, much the largest member, felt an increasing fear of being totally excluded from the most lucrative markets of Europe if it continued to stay outside the latter. In 1971 Britain and Denmark left EFTA to join the EEC, Norway having originally also agreed to switch but having its decision reversed by a plebiscite. Together with the Irish Republic which joined at the same time, the Six have thus become the Nine, and at the time of writing the absorption of three additional members, Greece, Spain and Portugal, is in the offing. Since the traditional neutrals, Switzerland, Austria and Sweden, are prevented by their obligation of neutrality from commitments that are partly political to one bloc, the enlarged Community will then embrace pretty much all of Europe west of the iron curtain.

It will be noticed that one aspect of economic integration which played a considerable part in the economic unification of Germany in the nineteenth century, not to mention the USA in the eighteenth, has so far eluded the drive to unification in postwar Europe: that is, a common currency. As the history of the interwar years showed, its significance in modern times is much greater than it might have been in past centuries, for currency manipulation not only provides a whole armoury for protectionist policies, but it is the strain on the currencies by which unbalances of trade are generally registered first, so that remedies along these lines come most readily to hand and have been permitted in emergencies in the postwar international economic agreements.

The enormous economic success in the early years of the Common Market kept the payments of all the six members in safe balance and allowed some of them to accumulate huge gold and foreign currency reserves out of their trading surpluses. The comfortable position hid the potential instability of a set of currencies kept at a fixed parity to each other, while internal price changes, payments balances and the attitude of currency speculators might differ widely between them. When the Italian lira was in trouble in 1963–4 aid was sought from the USA rather than the EEC partners, but the Council of Ministers of the EEC set up a 'Fiscal Policy Committee' in 1964. The next strain appeared in 1969, when France devalued unilaterally by 12·5 per cent without consulting its partners and the Deutschmark was allowed to drift upwards. By 1971, with further upward movements of both the Deutschmark and the

Netherlands guilder, while the Belgian franc was being held only by a dual market system, it was clear that the times of easy adjustment had passed. New parities were adopted in December of that year, but the circle of keeping constant relations between currencies subjected to differential strains could no longer be squared for any length of time. In a welter of linguistic constructs, from 'adjustable pegs' to 'crawling pegs' and a 'snake in the tunnel', what the member countries (together with others) have since then attempted to do is to permit variations in exchange values, but limit them in extent and reduce the element of surprise and unilateral action. The major achievement here was the European Monetary System (EMS), inaugurated after some delay in March 1979, under which eight of the nine members of the EEC (Great Britain excluding itself) undertook to limit fluctuations in their exchange rates to ± 2·25 per cent, or ± 6 per cent in the case of the Italian lira. In September of that year the Deutschmark was up-valued by 2 per cent and the Danish crown devalued by 3 per cent. It would not be unfair to say that in 1980 the idea of a common currency for the whole of the Common Market seems as far from realisation as ever, and without it there will exist a constant and at times critical source of strain on all its economic policies, including the obligation not to inhibit or discriminate in matters of trade. These strains will not be made any easier by the fact that there is not, and there cannot be, a common system of taxation either, except for certain forms of indirect taxation.

Meanwhile the other part of Europe, the countries of the Eastern bloc (with Yugoslavia uncertainly between the two camps), were moving in a parallel direction. In the early postwar years only the most minimal economic and commercial contacts existed between them. This was largely because their model was the Soviet Union, a large and potentially almost self-sufficient country which had carried through its industrialisation and transition to 'socialism' in virtual isolation from the outside world. Hence the blueprint 'plans' of each of these countries also envisaged a series of independent industrial and political revolutions, rather than being part of a worldwide sweep of revolutions such as some of the earlier Marxist leaders had dreamed of.

The impetus for greater integration came largely from the example in the West in an era of East–West cold war. It was in one of the most acrimonious phases of that war, in 1949, that the Council for Mutual Economic Assistance, commonly known as COMECON, was established by the Eastern nations. Even then, its very name suggests a much looser degree of integration than was being developed in the West, and its commercial links, let alone the extent of dovetailed economic or industrial planning, turned out to be extremely limited in extent. Part of the reason for this is that in controlled and planned economies the traditional Western measures such as protection or its abolition lose nearly all their significance as against the direction taken by planned trade, while labour migration, and still more the transfer of capital, are likely to be minimal if they are permitted at all. We must also remember the background of the long-standing national feuds and traditional hostility among several of these countries. Yet such integration as was achieved was important in principle, for it was part of a more far-reaching political and military association of these countries under the leadership of the Soviet Union.

The price for the relative lowering of barriers between the countries of Europe, and the enormous, and by past experience unimaginable, growth in output and economic welfare both East and West that accompanied it, was thus the raising of the barrier between the two halves of Europe – both a result and a precondition of the regional associations. That barrier was largely political, but it clearly affected economic relations also.

Freedom of labour migration is to all intents and purposes non-existent across the divide, marked by the horrors of high walls, barbed wire and armed watch-towers along much of its length. Capital movements are also little more than a trickle.

Trade, however, has picked up in recent years, and in some cases amounts to a larger share of foreign commerce of Eastern countries than trade among themselves. The realities of European economic needs have been allowed to reassert themselves, and will continue to do so as long as political necessity does not thwart them, as so often in the past. Significantly, though, there is no longer a simple trade pattern of manufactures moving from the advanced West, and food and some raw materials being the only saleable products of the East. On the contrary, many manufactured consumer goods and even some sophisticated capital goods are sold by Eastern countries into Western markets, while Western exports include agricultural surplus products and even wheat, mostly exported from North America. East–West trade therefore shows the same increasing refinement in the sense of an exchange of particular products rather than whole sweeps of product groups that we have traced in the trade among the Western advanced countries themselves.

7 Conclusion

There has been one constant theme running through the economic history of the past two centuries or more: the growing opportunities of economic integration over ever wider distances, and parallel with them the growing potential gains from using them. This has been largely a matter of technology: new technologies of transport lowering the costs of trade, but also, equally important, new technologies of production, allowing the use of previously unused natural resources, encouraging specialisation and frequently raising the minimum efficient size of the productive unit, so that ever larger markets become a necessity for efficient and low-cost production.

As a result, trade links and the interdependence of factors of production have steadily increased also, and whenever they were permitted to, have grown faster than output itself. One effect has been the expansion of the area over which trade is conducted. From the local exchange between village and market town, it became intra-regional, then a trade between neighbouring regions, and ultimately trade between each region and the world. All of these have existed side by side from time immemorial, but their relative weight has changed substantially in favour of the longer-distance exchange over our period.

93

Another effect, of equal importance, and related to changing supply as well as to rising demand associated with rising output, has been a concentration on more specialised trade, depending on distinctions by brand and minor shades of quality as well as between broad groups of commodities. The weight of trade has therefore shifted at least in part from an exchange, say, of food as against machinery, to cross-trade in the same commodity with slight differences in style or quality only. This is largely trade among European countries themselves. In 1909–13 some 65 per cent of European trade was with the rest of Europe, and in 1925–30, despite the virtual disappearance of Russia as a trading partner, it was still 61 per cent. Since the war the 'intra-trade' between the industrial countries has increased faster than any other section of world trade, and it is very largely a trade in manufactured products.

At the same time, while labour migration has yet again taken on a different aspect, as it has on several earlier occasions, it has been as large in quantity and importance as at any time in the past. Its main thrust has been of labour from the Mediterranean countries, including Italy, Spain, Portugal, Turkey, Cyprus and Yugoslavia, into the high-wage countries of Central and Western Europe. There has also been substantial East–West migration, but much of it, particularly within what was once Germany, has been politically determined. This migration, it should be noted, does not depend on customs unions, and is often weak within them, as in the EEC or the Nordic Union, but strong across their boundaries.

By contrast, capital has moved relatively little, at least within Europe. Instead, there has been a much greater degree of integration across frontiers *within* firms, as well as exchanges of components at different stages of manufacture.

Here the typical new form of enterprise is the multinational. As a production unit it may be scattered over many countries, so that while the firm may be German its product parts may be manufactured in Portugal and assembled in Britain. Movements of goods between branches are often undertaken at nominal or artificial prices for reasons of taxation. Commercial policies, as conceived by governments, are therefore sieved through the internal needs of the multinationals before they can actually affect trade on the ground, so that import and export figures, as well as tariff rates, lose much of their traditional meanings. The internal interconnections may be so close that it may not always be possible to determine what country the company as a whole belongs to, let alone the true origin of its products.

Even as between independent firms, the origins of components may have a wide international base, such as Japanese tubes in Dutch television sets, or Swiss components in Japanese watches. To some extent that was always true, and German machinery, for example, might always have had Swedish iron ore and Finnish timber in it, but this is now made much clearer as the sophistication of multi-stage manufacturing grows. Of course, designs, blueprints and patents which have always been international, have become totally interdependent across the national frontiers.

This, then, is the economic rationale: growing economic integration dictated by factors, prices, endowments, technological achievements and tastes. But parallel with it there is also a political rationale, which gives increasing powers, including growing powers over the economy, to the fervently independent and sovereign states and governments of Europe. We have seen that there have been phases when these two have tended in the same direction, to the benefit of both, and there have been other phases when the political authorities have found themselves in postures inhibiting economic integration, with disastrous results for both the political and the economic fortunes of Europe. But even if the general political posture is favourable to integration, as it has been in the past three decades and more, the logic of the state still largely pulls in the opposite direction. Heavily subsidised national industries, tax and social security schemes, even education, weights and measures, nomenclature, quality standards and a host of other governmental initiatives, necessary in complex industrial economies for the protection of society and to ensure progress, all tend to cut up the European economy into separate units shut off from each other. Since they exist, governments become the poles of attraction of all economic demands, hopes, intrigues and manoeuvres, and this in turn enhances their divisive functions and powers.

The aim of integrationists therefore has been, and must be, to turn the governments themselves into instruments of integration. In so far as integration has made headway, it has done so because the initiative has been shifted in that way, and in so far as it has been blocked, the cause is to be found in the same quarter. The citizens, as citizens, control both the economic and the political apparatus, but the reins are loose and long, and large organisations, including governments, have a tendency to take off on their own momentum irrespective of what the nominal ultimate controllers desire. The economic integration of Europe, Western Europe alone or both halves of it, has thus become a burning political issue and is bound to remain so.

Bibliography

Abel, Derryck (1945), *A History of British Tariffs*, London, Heath Cranton.
A useful history of the switch to protection in Britain.

Alexandrowicz, Charles Henry (1952), *International Economic Organisations*, London, Institute of World Affairs/Stevens.
Extensive, mostly factual account of the more important organisations, their origins, history and functions.

Ashley, Percy (1910), *Modern Tariff History: Germany, United States, France*, London, Murray, 2nd edn.
The standard history of modern tariffs in the three main industrial nations other than Britain. Factual, superficial, but reliable.

Ashworth, William (1952), *A Short History of the International Economy 1850–1950*, London, Longman.
A useful view of the unifying tendencies in the world economy.

Ballassa, Bela (1973), 'Monetary integration in the European Common Market', in A. Swoboda (ed.), *Europe and the Evolution of the International Monetary System*, Leyden, Sijthoff.
A very clear account of the complexities of monetary policies in the light of pressures on currencies from the Treaty of Rome onwards.

Ballassa, Bela (ed.) (1975), *European Economic Integration*, Amsterdam, North Holland Publishing Co.
Largely theoretical articles on the development and prospects of the EEC.

Barkin, Kenneth, D. (1970), *The Controversy over German Industrialization 1890–1902*, Chicago, Chicago University Press.
A very detailed account of the debate and its (largely academic) protagonists over whether Germany should retain its agrarian base or become more industrialised.

Berrill, Kenneth (1960), 'International Trade and the rate of economic growth', *Economic History Review*, 12, pp. 351–9.
A brief theoretical discussion.

Bonn, Moritz J. (1938), *The Crumbling of Empire. The Disintegration of World Economy*, London, Allen & Unwin.
Relates changes in world trade to the build-up and decline of colonial empires.

Cameron, Rondo E. (1961), *France and the Economic Development of Europe 1800–1914*, Princeton, NJ, Princeton University Press.
Detailed history of the involvement of French capital in foreign railway and other investment. A seminal study.

Camps, Miriam (1967), *European Unification in the Sixties*, London, Oxford University Press.
One of the best of a large number of books on this theme.

Cassel, Gustav (1936), *The Downfall of the Gold Standard*, Oxford, Clarendon Press.
A much-used contemporary study, providing a good insight into the motivations and pressures at the time.

Clough, S. B. (1964), *France: A History of National Economics 1789–1939*, New York, Octagon.
A study of economic policies, including protectionist and free-trade doctrines, in France. A good summary of the secondary literature in this complex field.

Condliffe, J. B. (1951), *The Commerce of Nations*, London, Allen & Unwin.
Standard historical account of the growth of world trade.

Dawson, W. H. (1964), *Protection in Germany*, London, King.
A somewhat hostile but reliable account.

De Beers, John S. (1941–2), 'Tariff aspects of a federal union', *Quarterly Journal of Economics*, 66, pp. 49–92.

In part a discussion of the interplay of a (political) federal union and its economic consequences.

Deutsch Karl, and Eckstein, Alexander (1961), 'National industrialization and the declining share of the international economic sector', *World Politics*, 13, pp. 267–99.
Typical for the prediction of a falling share of world trade, falsified by events.

Dunham, A. L. (1930), *The Anglo-French Treaty of Commerce in 1860 and the Progress of the Industrial Revolution in France*, Ann Arbor, Mich., University of Michigan Press.
A major work, though a little dated now, on the most significant commercial treaty of the nineteenth century.

Ferenczi, Imre, and Willcox, Walter, F. (1929, 1931), *International Migrations*, New York, NBER, 2 vols.
Vast statistical and historical compendium for migration in most countries or regions.

Hobson, C. K. (1914), *The Export of Capital*, London, Constable.
Useful contemporary account of the foreign investment of Britain and some other countries.

Friedman, Philip (1974), *The Impact of Trade Destruction on National Incomes: A study of Europe 1924–1938*, Gainesville, Fla., University of Florida Press.
Very good short account of the antecedents and course of European economic disintegration in the interwar years. Less successful econometric attempt to count the costs.

Gaedicke, Herbert, and Von Eynern, Gert (1933), *Die Produktionswirtschaftliche Integration Europas*, Berlin, Junker & Dünnhaupt.
An early statistical attempt to trace the trade relationships within Europe and their economic significance.

General Agreement on Tariffs and Trade (1964), *The Role of GATT in Relation to Trade and Development*, Geneva, GATT.
Official survey including useful data.

Gordon, Margaret S. (1941), *Barriers to World Trade. A Study of Recent Commercial Practice*, New York, Macmillan.
Useful account of the protectionist policies of various kinds in the 1930s.

99

Grampp, William (1965), *Economic Liberalism*, New York, Random House, 2 vols.
Puts the free trade theory into its classic setting as part of a wider doctrine of economic liberalism.

Haas, Ernst B. (1958), *The Uniting of Europe: Political, Social and Economic Forces 1950–1957*, Stanford, Calif., California University Press.
A critical view, reflecting attitudes at the beginning of the EEC.

Hallstein, Walter (1972), *Europe in the Making*, London, Allen & Unwin; 1st German edn. 1969.
Mainly about the Common Market, by one of its architects.

Heimann, Hanns (ed.) (1926), *Europäische Zollunion*, Berlin, Reimar Hobbing.
A set of papers favouring and discussing the economic consequences of a European customs union.

Henderson, William Otto (1959), *The Zollverein*, London, Frank Cass; 1st edn. 1933.
The standard work in the English language. Highly factual, and in the tradition of seeing the Zollverein as a triumph of far-seeing Prussian statesmanship.

Henderson, William Otto (1962), *The Genesis of the Common Market*, London, Frank Cass.
Highlights certain antecedent movements that built up the tradition in which the Common Market was possible, e.g. the Zollverein, river and maritime agreements, the gold standard. Factual, rather elementary.

Hilgerd, Folke (1943), 'The Case for Multilateral Trade', *American Economic Review*, supplement, 33, pp. 393–407.
A plea for multilateral trade on the ground that the bilateral agreements of the 1930s reduced incomes as well as trade for all nations.

Kaser, Michael (1965), *Comecon. Integration Problems of the Planned Economies*, London, Royal Institute of Economic Affairs/Oxford University Press.
The early standard work. Tends to stress the low level of integration and trade between the countries of Eastern Europe.

Kindleberger, C. P. (1962), *Foreign Trade and the National Economy*, New Haven, Conn., Yale University Press.

Historical and theoretical discussion. Contains useful explanations of economic terms used frequently.

Lambi, Ivo Nikolai (1963), *Free Trade and Protection in Germany 1868–1879*, Wiesbaden, Fritz Stein.
A very detailed account of the arguments, the economic interests involved and the political constellation as a background to the triumph and defeat of free trade in Bismarck's Germany.

Lambrinidis, John (1965), *The Structure, Function and Law of a Free Trade Area: The European Free Trade Association*, London, Stevens.
Useful factual and theoretical survey.

League of Nations (1942), *The Network of World Trade*, Geneva, League of Nations.
Useful statistical account.

League of Nations, Economic, Financial and Transit Department (1942), *Commercial Policy in the Interwar Period: International Proposals and National Policies*, Geneva, League of Nations.
A systematic and factual account of conventions, aggreements and meetings, nominally neutral but in fact strongly favouring free trade.

League of Nations, Economic, Financial and Transit Department (1945), *Industrialization and World Trade*, Geneva, League of Nations.
A study covering the 1870s to the 1930s on changes in the main flow of world trade, related to economic development in some major regions.

Machlup, Fritz (1977), *A History of Thought on Economic Integration*, London, Macmillan.
A vast compendium of economic theories, movements to integration and biographies of the leading 'Europeans'. A mine of information on a variety of things.

Maizels, Alfred (1963), *Industrial Growth and World Trade*, Cambridge, Cambridge University Press.
A large-scale study of world production and trade in manufactures, 1899–1959. A pioneer study, indispensable for an understanding of the relationship between economic development and international trade.

Myrdal, Gunnar (1956), *An International Economy: Problems and Prospects*, London, Routledge & Kegan Paul.
A complex book, contrasting the historical experience of integration within countries with international integration.

Pollard, Sidney (1973), 'Industrialization and the European economy', *Economic History Review*, 26, pp. 631–48.
An attempt to see European industrialization as a single continent-wide process.

Pollard, Sidney (1974), *European Economic Integration 1815–1970*, London, Thames & Hudson.
Brief historical account, in terms of technology and economic sectors.

Pryor, Frederic L. (1963), *The Communist Foreign Trade System: The Other Common Market*, Cambridge, Mass., MIT Press.
A highly critical survey.

Renouvin, Pierre (1949), *L'idée de fédération européenne dans la pensée politique du XIXe siècle*, Oxford, Clarendon Press.
Lecture on political idealism.

Rist, Marcel (1956), 'Une expérience française de libération des échanges au XIXe siècle: Le traité de 1860', *Revue d'économie politique*, 66, pp. 908–57.
Detailed account of the treaty, its antecedents and some consequences.

Roepke, Wilhelm (1950), *International Economic Disintegration*, London, Hodge, 3rd edn; 1st end. 1942.
A passionate denunciation of economic policies leading to the break-up of the European economy in the interwar years.

Rose, J. Holland (1916), *Nationalism as a Factor in Modern History*, London, Rivington.
A wide-ranging historical study of the principle of nationality. An excellent introduction.

Salter, Sir Arthur (ed.) (1927), *The Economic Consequences of the League: The World Economic Conference*, London, Routledge.
A set of papers on the antecedents and results of the 1927 World Economic Conference, including the official report adopted by it.

Tinbergen, Jan (1965), *International Economic Integration*, Amsterdam, Elsevier, 2nd edn.
Largely theoretical, but providing useful statistics.

Vaughan, Richard (1976), *Post-War Integration in Europe*, London, Edward Arnold.

Reliable account of post-1945 movements, with a short historical introduction.

Vaughan, Richard (1979), *Twentieth-Century Europe. Paths to Unity*, London, Croom Helm.
A useful quarry for data on movements towards European unity from the early nineteenth century.

Viner, Jacob (1950), *The Customs Union Issue*, New York, Carnegie Endowment.
The classic work on the economic theory of customs union.

Walsh, A. E., and Paxton, John (1968), *The Structure and Development of the Common Market*, London, Hutchinson.
A good factual work.

Weithase, Hugo (1895), *Geschichte des Weltpostvereins*, Strasbourg, Heitz.
Standard history of the Universal Postal Union.

Woytinsky, Vladimir (1926), *Die Vereinigten Staaten von Europa*, Berlin, Dietz.
A plea for integration on political and economic grounds.

INDEX